*Something of Myself
and Others*

First published in 2013 by
Liberties Press
140 Terenure Road North | Terenure | Dublin 6W
Tel: +353 (1) 4055740
www.libertiespress.com | info@libertiespress.com

Trade enquiries to Gill & Macmillan Distribution
Hume Avenue | Park West | Dublin 12
T: +353 (1) 500 9534 | F: +353 (1) 500 9595 | E: sales@gillmacmillan.ie

Distributed in the UK by
Turnaround Publisher Services
Unit 3 | Olympia Trading Estate | Coburg Road | London N22 6TZ
T: +44 (0) 20 8829 3000 | E: orders@turnaround-uk.com

Distributed in the United States by
IPM | 22841 Quicksilver Dr | Dulles, VA 20166

ISBN: 978-1-907593-82-6

2 4 6 8 10 9 7 5 3 1

A CIP record for this title is available from the British Library.

Cover design by Fergal Condon
Internal design by Liberties Press

Something of Myself and Others

Mary Kenny

In some respects we make our own life; in others we submit to the life that others have made for us.

George Sand

Contents

*For Marjorie Wallace, Countess Skarbek, who will kill me
if I don't mention her. With love and gratitude.*

Author's Note

An autobiography is supposed to be a straight narrative of the author's life; George Orwell says that no autobiography is plausible unless it contains something disgraceful and shameful about the writer's story. A memoir, by contrast, is a discreetly selective tranche of what the writer cares to remember, or chooses to put on the record. I like that idea better. As there is no copyright in titles, I was tempted to use the title of Katharine Whitehorn's memoir, *Selective Memory*, which is disarmingly pleasing in implying selective amnesia. I also considered the late Seán MacRéamoinn's witty description of his life being like an Irish census return: *Broken Down by Sex, Age and Religion*. But instead I've chosen the somewhat reserved title first used by Rudyard Kipling in his short recollection, *Something of Myself*.

The material here contains *something* of myself. I have grown to know my capacities and limitations, and I know I find it difficult to write about myself in a direct, consistent or frank way; I can only do so elliptically, by bringing my recollections to a range of anecdotes or experiences, by focusing on a place or an event, and by writing about other people, or particular situations, which parts of my life touch. (I also write best about people when they are dead – perhaps I am a natural obituarist either because life cannot be summed up until the final curtain, or because death frees you to reflect upon a life more honestly. When my friends die before me, I write about them: if I die before them, they will presumably write about me. That's fine.)

And so this is a kind of ragbag of memoirs, experiences, dead friends, family members, and episodes. I hope that part of it might entertain, part of it might inform, and part might stand as a picture of a generation of Irish women born (for the most part) in the 1940s, and coming of age in the

1960s; part might bear witness to my experience as a family carer.

Some of the pieces in this collection have previously appeared in print, usually in a shorter version, mostly in the *Irish Independent*, the *Guardian* and the *Daily Mail*. As mentioned above, I myself published an earlier – shorter and in many parts different – version of this collection, but people were kind enough to say they found it readable, and different people liked different aspects.

I would like to thank my friend of forty years, and co-grandmother (we have the blessings of grandchildren in common) Valerie Grove for reading this earlier version and making literate and useful comments. I would also like to thank Sean O'Keeffe, the publisher of Liberties Press and Clara Phelan, as editor, who has been patient, understanding and hugely efficient. And my agent Louise Greenberg who is always a source of wisdom and support.

Part One
Adventures in the Media Trade

An Apprenticeship
I blagged my way into journalism

When I told my mother I was going into journalism, she looked dismayed.

'Oh darling – women journalists are *awful*. So cynical, and such hard drinkers.' She was, of course, right.

There is such a difference between the world of journalism that I entered in the 1960s, and the profession as it stands today, that it might as well be a different world. But it was a different world and a different century, and life has always changed with the passage of time, and that is the natural order of things.

Journalism was not, in those days, an entirely respectable profession: it was not regarded as a profession at all.

That journalism was a trade, not a profession, was emphasised to me by an old Fleet Street hand when I was an aspiring reporter. 'We don't want any of your hoity-toity Varsity types here,' he said. 'Graduates with their fancy ideas! No, we want keen lads and lasses who came up the hard way, and know about the bread and butter issues.'

Journalism certainly would not have been mentioned at my convent school as a career choice – not that there was a great deal about career choices beyond much praise for Guinnesses, the porter-makers, regarded as Dublin's best employers. (They didn't hire Catholics at management level at the time, but that was not a source of grievance. The Irish State was Catholic, but business was often Protestant, and that was an accepted convention – even accepted as fair balance in the division of labour.)

Indeed, 'journalism' was used as a word of disparagement by one of my English teachers, Mother Catherine, who spoke nostalgically about her missionary time in Mauritius and looked like Alastair Sim in the St Trinian's movies. After I had put my most earnest efforts into a school essay, Mother Catherine wrote, in scarlet ink at the bottom: 'This is not English prose, though I suppose it might pass as some kind of cheap journalism.'

Ah, self-fulfilling prophesies! That was to be my fate! 'Some kind of cheap journalism.' I cannot look back on my schooldays and say that I ever received a word of encouragement from anyone at my convent school - this being the Loreto College, St Stephen's Green in Dublin. Why didn't my family send me to the Holy Child in Killiney, like Maeve Binchy? Or Mount Anville, like Mary Robinson? I wonder if I could get a misery memoir out of this source of deprivation?

Back in the 1960s, people often drifted into journalism by hanging around the pubs that newspapermen frequented in an attempt to pick up a bit of freelance work. London was more codified than Dublin: there was a trade union 'closed shop' in London, and it was a bit tougher to get a National Union of Journalists' card. But people managed. There were always ways and means. And as the 1960s wore on, there were more graduates entering journalism, especially from Oxford and Cambridge, a matchless field for making connections.

Yet, as late as the 1990s, the editor of the *Daily Mail*, Paul Dacre – a sweet man, despite a reputation for robust language and tough attitudes – told me he still wasn't sure whether graduates or non-graduates made the best journalists. 'Graduates have a better education, but does their time at university take the edge off their eagerness? Non-graduates are hungrier.'

I suppose I started in journalism feeling hungry, indeed.

* * *

I really always wanted to be a playwright – and I have not given up on this teenage dream – but when I was a penuriously paid and not very successful au pair girl in Paris in the early 1960s, I came to realise that you could earn some money in journalism. When I sent an article to the *Evening Press* in Dublin, the features editor, Sean McCann (father of the novelist Colum McCann) not only accepted it, but he paid me three pounds for it. Had journalism been a profession, like medicine or the law, the fee would have been remitted in guineas – three pounds and three shillings.

The article I submitted was a description of the great care and endless trouble a French family takes in planning and preparing and savouring elaborate meals (in contrast to the simplicity of Irish life, where you had an egg for your tea, followed, possibly, by a slice of barn brack.) I was, by instinct or luck, with the spirit of the age: 1962 was the beginning of the food revolution in Britain and Ireland, when Elizabeth David was introducing the art of Mediterrean cooking to all those who had previously had an egg or a sausage for their evening meal. Forthwith it would be avocados with shrimps.

In Paris, I began to hang out in the café-pubs of Montparnasse with two Irish journalists, Peter Lennon and Joe Carroll – tarrying together in the Falstaff, the Dome, La Coupole. Peter Lennon wrote for the *Guardian* and was often seen drinking with a craggy-faced man who talked about cricket: this was Samuel Beckett.

I didn't have the slightest interest in writing about food, but I thought everything French was superior: diligently had I imbibed my lessons at the *Alliance Francaise*, where I was told: '*Chaque homme civilise a deux patries – la sienne, et la France.*'

I also imbibed, probably instinctively, the lesson that journalism is often about opportunity – and opportunism. When you see the opportunity, you take it. I had left school at sixteen and was making my own way in the world. Indeed I walked away from my convent school with the farewell words from Mother Annunciata, the reverend mother, ringing in my ears – 'You must now sink or swim by your own efforts'. I knew I had to grasp whatever chances I could.

But besides opportunity you also need, as the great French renaissance poet Joachim du Bellay pointed out in another context, friends at court. You need someone who will publish you, encourage you and help you out. Sean McCann constantly did that, once sending me an urgent telegram about an available spot in the *Irish Press* for a piece about an Irish girl abroad. 'This is important,' he wrote. I posted the piece and it was duly published, looking very impressive in a national newspaper. I think I was nineteen at the time, and I believe the reward was a glistening fiver, or its equivalent in francs.

Today every young journalist has a degree, and they are all the better-informed for it. In many respects, the standards of journalism are higher and I'm greatly impressed by the trainee journalists who approach me for interviews about past times in the media. Whether the trade is as much fun as it was in those rackety days of my youth is for the next generation to decide. It is certainly more bourgeois, and so respectable that it has become a much sought-after profession. Some of the grumpier old men would also say it has become more 'feminised'. But I do not believe a schoolteacher today would disparage a pupil's essay with scornful words about 'some kind of cheap journalism'.

Yet in entering any trade or profession, there is talent, there is training, there is opportunity and there is temperament. I have known people who had the talent to be great journalists, but not the temperament. The temperament means taking the knocks. The editor of the *Evening Standard*, Charles Wintour (father of the now more famous Anna Wintour, the world's best-known and most exacting fashionista, and also the inspiration for Meryl Streep's character in *The Devil Wears Prada*) my most formative mentor, would hold it as a principle with any application: 'If you can't stand the heat, don't come into the kitchen'.

I talked my way into getting hired at the London *Evening Standard* in the 1960s. After drifting to London from Paris, I had done secretarial work at the *Guardian* (I was a useless secretary, rather as I had been a hopeless au pair – I failed at a lot of things in the process of struggling to earn my living), working for the deputy editor, Gerard Fay, a kind but melancholy man whose father, Frank, had been a co-founder of the Abbey Theatre in Dublin. He thus had a soft spot for the Irish. 'Go to Charles Wintour at the *Evening Standard*,' he advised. And so I did. Mr Wintour asked me to give him one good reason why he should engage me: 'Well, you won't know what you're missing if you don't,' I replied. 'I can't resist that,' replied the editor who was sometimes known as 'Chilly Charlie'(Ms Wintour did not lick her famous *froideur* off the stones, as the Irish expression has it.) And through boldness, I had a job.

Charles Wintour could be chilly in manner but he was a dedicated editor and a great teacher. My early years at the *Evening Standard* under the tutelage of Charles Wintour became in effect, my university. I learned everything I needed to know about the world from 1966 to 1968 under his tutelage, and the first lesson has stayed with me.

I was despatched off to interview Earl Attlee, for it was his eightieth birthday. My first query, in response to the assignment, was: 'Who's Earl Attlee?' If I am ever tempted to deplore the ignorance of younger generations today who might say, 'Who was General Eisenhower? Who was Siobhán McKenna?' I call to mind my ignorance in not knowing of Clement Attlee, the great post-war British prime minister, steward of the Welfare State and, as I learned much later, a steadfast holiday-maker in Ireland, where his wife would drive – atrociously – across the country in their Morris Minor with only one unarmed, diffident plain-clothes police officer for security.

Attlee lived in a retired apartment in the Temple, London EC, in 1966. He was always taciturn and by this time, very deaf, and I was completely untutored. But his courteous manners and my eagerness produced some pleasant enough exchanges and the interview went into the paper. Although feminism taught our generation to complain of lack of equal opportunities there was, if I am to be honest, a compensatory gallantry that older men generally showed to young women of twenty-two, and that often advanced us in other ways.

* * *

I worked, then, on Londoner's Diary at the *Standard*. The Diary traditionally recruited languid young men just down from Oxford – in this department, a university degree was more than acceptable, particularly if Oxford, and sometimes Cambridge, provided the budding journo with good connections. (Oxford was considered superior to Cambridge for social connections: Oxford being the political world, Cambridge the scientific one.) The languid young men also quite often came from upper-class families with social connections. And not all of them were languid – Max Hastings, who was part of my intake, was always frantically hyper-energetic and drivingly ambitious (significantly, he had dropped out of Oxford because he was in a hurry to get on with his career, and he had contempt for the clever public schoolboys he had known at Charterhouse). But he came with those useful social connections – his mother had been a very successful journalist called Anne Scott-James, and his father a national figure on TV, Macdonald Hastings.

The media often works in stereotypes and if the cap fits to your profit, you wear it. I was surrounded by these former public schoolboys and I was cast in the role – which I more than readily embraced – of the Wild Irish Girl. There is always a vacancy in any organisation, for a Head Boy, a Wild Rebel, a Bossy Battleaxe, for a Den Mother and an Alpha Male. This is the stuff on which soap operas are built.

The remit on Londoner's Diary was simply to report on everything that was happening in London. One day it was Earl Attlee, the next day it was, 'there's some weird Japanese bird who is showing an exhibition of her photographs of bottoms – go to it': and that was London's introduction to Yoko Ono. A 'pocket profile' might be required of Tom Wolfe, or Marlene Dietrich, or Marlon Brando, or Francois Truffaut, and you would be dispatched to the Savoy, or the Connaught, or the Dorchester or some film set at Elstree and file a piece by mid-day. The newspaper interview was expanding in style and space, and there were some brilliant young practitioners of the art of the interview: Maureen Cleave, Jilly Cooper, Valerie Grove (then Jenkins), Hunter Davies, Ray Connolly. Show business interviews were less controlled than they are today: in the late 1990s, I was despatched to interview Pierce Brosnan at the Shelbourne Hotel in Dublin, and while he was amicable and professional, the format was conducted in the shape of a queue at the dentist's. A dozen interviewers would be lined up and each would be allocated twenty to thirty minutes each. Hard work for the star, but thin pickings, too, for the interviewer: a fruitful interview needs time, and even relaxation. Barry Norman has written about interviewing Richard Burton back in the 1960s. The format was they went on a three-day bender together. I remember interviewing the graceful Deborah Kerr at the Connaught Hotel in Mayfair in the 1970s, and we lingered for some time over a leisurely afternoon tea, with no publicity agents or other minders harrying the conversation.

On Londoner's Diary, we were expected to ring up distinguished or

famous people and ask them for a quote, often posing footlingly embar-
rassing questions at eight o'clock in the morning – for it was held as a self-
evident truth that the way to get a straight (or candid) answer out of
anyone is to telephone them at 8 AM, or earlier (this has been called 'the
Gestapo technique').

People just emerging from sleep will blurt out anything. I was once
obliged to telephone the Archbishop of Canterbury at that hour and ask
him – for God's sake! – 'what side do you sleep on, my Lord?' His valet had
presumably brought him to the telephone saying the press was anxious to
speak to him, possibly anticipating some major ecclesiastical crisis, and
then he had this nitwit of a young reporter asking him tomfooleries.
Michael Ramsey showed not only Christian forebearance, but sweetness
and light beyond the call of duty, and entered a silly conversation with
great courtesy. I have always thought fondly of him ever since.

Although there were star feature-writers, there were fewer women in
journalism when I started out, and some of those who were successful
could be tougher than the men. There was an awesomely renowned
reporter at the *Evening Standard* called Anne Sharpley – long gone to her
eternal reward – and she really was an ace journalist. She would do her
research carefully in advance of any assignment: she would consult vari-
eties of coniferous and deciduous trees at the British Museum just so she
could report that 'the Queen stood under the banga-banga tree as she
opened the ceremony.' The Queen, and Princess Margaret, and Princess
Alexandra, spent a remarkable amount of time going around the world
lowering the Union Jack in Commonwealth countries about to step forward into independence, and there was always a phalanx of reporters to
accompany the royal party.

Anne was, in her heyday, so tough that no one could compete with her.
Her idea of beating the competition was vandalising a public phone box
after she had finished filing – the better to thwart the competing newspaper and cause them to miss an edition (according to the legend about her
matchless reportage of the funeral of Sir Winston Churchill). In contrast to
my Ma's prediction, Anne had no interest in drink, and that, possibly made
her even sharper. The men sometimes resented her gritty sobriety and felt

that it gave her an unfair advantage, somehow – as did her sex. 'Oh, she always gets the story all right,' I was told by a male reporter. 'That's because when the men are drinking at the local taverna, on a foreign trip, she goes off and sleeps with the Fascist police chief.' This may be quite unfair to Anne Sharpley's memory, though she did once advise me, when I was embarking on an overseas assignment, 'always sleep with the Reuters' man, doll'. Why so? 'Because the newsdesk checks your copy against Reuters, and you'll have filed before him.'

She was altogether a superb reporter, but some of the life lessons I took from La Sharpley were distinctly the wrong values. Her advice about 'sleeping with the Reuters' man' would, today, be considered wildly unethical, from every point of view, including, possibly, plagiarism: and we no longer entertain the idea that women use sexual favours to further their ambitions.

Anne was, probably, too tough. In middle life she had a kind of nervous breakdown, and emerged from it a dedicated feminist, which had never previously interested her, and an acerbic critic of some of the values of the newspaper trade.

There were aspects of journalism that I found cringingly uncomfortable, and nerve-wranglingly anxious: frightening, too. Getting that story, or failing to get it was terrifying. But there was always a remedy for the anxieties of the trade: drink. Yes, I learned to drink like a typical journalist – just as my Ma had foretold – like a traditional journalist, and that was a disaster.

Acquiring the drinking habit...

I began drinking in Paris as a teenager, but it was usually a modest glass of rosé in a Montparnasse café, an essential part of my fantasy of being a Left Bank intellectual and living in an artist's garret. (Actually, I did live in a garret: it was called a maid's room, given to me by some adorable Irish-Americans, the Quinns, in exchange for some babysitting.)

That gave me a taste for drinking, and the pleasant experience of mild inebriation. But it wasn't until I became a journalist in London in 1966 that I became, as the Irish say so euphemistically, 'fond' of the drink.

Drinking was tolerated in journalism – both in London and in Dublin: it was even regarded with a certain heroic approach. Sam White, the then legendary Paris correspondent of the *Evening Standard*, religiously repaired to the Crillon hotel each morning at 11 AM, there to consume a bottle of champagne. '*Si on demande pour moi, je serai au bar,*' was his legendary saying.

But there was one proviso with journalistic drinking: you must not miss a deadline.

When President Kennedy was assassinated in Dallas in 1963, the story broke around 6 PM British time, and the best-known political columnist for the *Daily Express* – who knew much about American politicals – had long departed for the local hostelries. A junior reporter was deputed to comb the pubs and taverns of Fleet Street, and at last found him in The Punch: he was too legless to write, for his fingers kept sticking between the interstices of the typewriter. He recovered his reputation – by quitting the booze – but the legend of the night JFK died remained as a warning. Drink as much as you like – but file.

The aim was to drink heroically, but to be able to hold it heroically too. I suffered under the delusion that I could drink any man under the table, but the truth was nearer to the Dorothy Parker witticism: 'One more drink and I'll be under the host.'

Why did journalists in those days drink so much? My husband, who was inordinately fond of pub culture – perhaps the only place he really felt he could be his true self – said that drinking cordially helped to overcome shyness. It was held as an important principle (by my first mentor, Charles Wintour) that 'a journalist must go out': he, or she, must frequent gregarious places, meet people, listen to gossip, make contacts. A shy journalist would have to drink to overcome the normal inhibitions of social discourse. I'm not sure that I drank out of shyness – I certainly wasn't shy as a young person – it was more that I liked the sensation, and the way it released my natural inclinations to recklessness and risk-taking.

But I also warmed to the camerardie of the pubs. I had a circle of pals. Like an orphan who found a warm foster home, the bar gave me a collegiality, just like those privileged young people who had gone to university. I now think with some fondness of El Vino in London and the Pearl Bar in Dublin, and the sparkling conversations I listened to, and participated in, in those watering-holes.

In London, there was a portrait of Madame Veuve Clicquot, the champagne widow, under which the doyen of opera and theatre critics of the time, Philip Hope-Wallace, would sit. The younger journos would sit around and hear good conversation and drink decent champagne. Women were not permitted to stand at the bar and order, but that never troubled me (I considered a protest carried out against this to be 'bourgeois' – the Marxist dismssive phrase for a gesture considered unserious, and not applicable to the working class – I'll say!). I once read that the tradition among the Beduoin is for the younger people to sit in a circle listening to the lore and tales of the elders, and thus did memory and tradition get passed on, and it was something like that. Philip was a homosexual – he wouldn't, I think, have described himself as 'gay' – who had worked for the *Times* and the *Guardian*, and belonged to a generation and a class of Englishmen who were in many respects more 'European' than those who subsequently waxed lyrical about the EU: he spoke French, Italian and German with ease, and had been to university at Heidelberg.

Glamorous foreign correspondents such as James Cameron (not the movie director) would sometimes be among the group. Cameron, who had started life as a poor Scotsman, had once filled in an expenses claim which read: 'To hire of camel – £500.' He transmitted tales of Lord Beaverbrook, the press baron who had died in 1964, but whose aura still hung over his newspapers. Beaverbrook was an eccentric (but a crafty wielder of power) who would not allow the word 'cancer' to appear in his newspapers, as he thought it was unlucky death by cancer was always 'from a long illness', and death by cancer after much treatment was 'a long illness, bravely borne' – euphemisms that are still invoked today.

In Dublin, where I took a job with the *Irish Press* in 1969, there were hilarious conversations at the Pearl Bar, where the journalist-scholar Seán MacRéamoinn would talk brilliantly about the difference between 'P' Celtic and 'Q' Celtic (how Scots and Irish Gaelige divides from Welsh, Manx and Breton), and Maeve Binchy first impressed me as a woman who could truly scintillate in competitive male company, telling stories that would have the men laughing uproariously. Maeve could also hold a prodigeous amount of drink without actually getting drunk.

With my late friend Mary Cummins, who wrote for the *Irish Times*, I once counted up how much we had imbibed in one twenty-four hour session. (Our offices were near enough to bars for quick entrances and exits.) First 'snifter' at 11 AM (large gin and tonic). Lunch: two gin and tonics followed by a bottle and a half of wine each. 'Snifter' at around 5 PM – a couple of gins (or vodkas), and then back to work. 7 PM: pub session with pals – often wine in the evening. 9 PM, supper with lashings of vino. 11 PM to 3 AM: postprandials consisting of brandies, whiskey sours, crème de menthes, and whatever else we could lay our hands on.

Oh yes, later we paid the price, for it led us up many a wrong path, and indeed much misery. Later again we got sober only with self-help groups. But the drinking had been wild, crazy and madcap, and for a very brief period, rapturous.

And I loved the company it involved. The company and the stories and the talk and the utter conviviality, and that was, for me, part of journalism in those days. Ma's words were prophetic.

Journalistic Ethics
An introduction

I look back on my early journalistic career with a somewhat rueful feeling. I sometimes blush now, to think of my brattishness. And in all honesty, I cannot recall any great discourses about 'ethics'. You did what you could get away with.

It was September 1967 and I was sent to New York by the London *Evening Standard*. I had a fabulous week there staying with my sister Ursula and her flatmate Elizabeth Nohilly on the Upper East Side (73rd Street between 2nd and 3rd Avenues). The *Evening Standard* man in New York, Leo Armati, showed me the town, in the days when foreign corre-spondents had lavish expense accounts (Lord Beaverbrook regarded it as a point of honour that his overseas representatives should be seen to be grand, and did not balk at paying for a bathful of champagne for His Man in Berlin). Leo took me to Sardi's, where we had the usual three-Martini-lunch, a bill of fare since immortalised in *Mad Men*.

The assignment was a hoot. I was to travel back from New York on the old *Queen Mary* luxury cruise liner, built on the Clyde in 1936 and now heading for retirement: this would be her last voyage between New York and Southampton. And the night before the ship sailed, there was a party on board – the *Queen Mary* still in dock.

There was a famous Fleet Street reporter at the time called Nick Tomalin (subsequently, his wife, Claire, was to become more famous than he as a historical biographer) whom we all thought defined journalism. Nick wrote that the qualities needed for a successful journalist were 'rat-like cunning, a plausible manner and a little literary ability'. Did I fulfil all three? I certainly had, as a young woman, a vixen-like cunning and I was sometimes unscrupulous in my ambitions. (Only later did 'Catholic guilt' kick in, and I began to brood about questions of ethics.)

On board the *Queen Mary*'s dockside party was a glittery array of nobs and various celebrities, as well as the British Foreign Secretary at the time, Mr George Brown. George Brown was a decent enough old cove: he had come up through the ranks of working-class self-improvement, attending working men's colleges and obtaining an apprenticeship in retailing at John Lewis as a fur salesman. He had joined the Labour Party in South London as a boy and became a successful trade union official.

In the early 1960s, there had been a sharp contest between himself and Harold Wilson for the leadership of the Labour Party. Wilson won – he probably had the edge because Brown had a reputation for not being a safe pair of hands when under the influence of alcohol. Although some wiseacres said that 'George Brown drunk is a better man than Harold Wilson sober'. Lady Violet Bonham-Carter, a scion of the establishment, described Brown as 'often . . . a drunken boor – rude, clumsy, devoid of finesse or subtlety, but an honest and loyal man', whereas Wilson was very able and clever but 'universally distrusted'.

Brown had become Foreign Secretary in 1966. He tried to push the Americans to withdraw honourably from Vietnam, and was a strong advocate of Britain joining what was then the Common Market, in the face of General de Gaulle's repeated rebuffs. But George often seemed to be in hot water, one way or the other, and the media took malicious glee in highlighting his gaffes. Harold Wilson and his 'kitchen cabinet' were also secretly briefing against Brown – 'twas ever thus in politics.

And so there I was at the *Queen Mary* party, aged twenty-three, wearing a mini-skirt and knocking back the champagne. When the orchestra starts up, I approach Her Majesty's Foreign Secretary and boldly invite him to dance with me. He concurs – men of his vintage weren't publicly rude to apparently pleasant young women. The dance at the time was an inchoate and ill-defined general jiggle called the frug, and as George and I frugged together, I made flattering conversation and asked him how he was enjoying life in his wonderful ministry.

He growled in a mildly paranoid way, saying that he 'wasn't going to let those buggers grind him down . . . they were all against him, and plotting his downfall and they had it in for him.' He was clearly extremely cross with the political scene at Westminster: he had had a few drinks and he was being indiscreet. But he wasn't to know I was a reporter and, naturally, I didn't tell him.

I stored all this up in my calculating little opportunistic brain – my husband later nicknamed me 'Becky O'Sharp' – and as soon as the frug was over, I went straight to the transatlantic telephone and transmitted every word poor George Brown had said to me. The *Evening Standard* was thrilled to pieces, and splashed the story all over the front page in the early edition: GEORGE FRUGS THE NIGHT AWAY. That the word frug sounded vaguely rude was an enhancement to the header. George was subsequently photographed, at the same event, frugging with a rather more generously-endowed lady, whose bosom he appeared to be peering down (actually his eyes were closed) and then all the papers had the story.

What heartless creatures we were! George Brown was making a damn fool of himself again and it was a fine splash for the front page. When I got back to London later, I was even more delighted to be called 'The Mata Hari of Fleet Street'.

George offered his resignation by and by – he was always offering his resignation – and it was accepted six months later, in March 1968. He never returned to office. The *Queen Mary* frugging story wasn't the only episode that brought him down, but it was a contributory factor to 'the character issue'.

His end was sad. In 1982 he walked out on his wife, of more than forty years, Sophie, and set up home with his secretary. Equally unexpectedly, he became a Roman Catholic. More predictably, he died of liver failure, in 1985, aged seventy-one.

Nick Tomalin, who gave us our precepts of ratlike cunning, a plausible manner and a little literary ability, was himself killed in the Yom Kippur war in 1973. Very unratlike, he had bravely gone right to the front line to get the story.

Reporting the French Revolution
– *of 1968*

It was 1968 – the year of students' revolts – and in Maytime, we got to hear that things were about to get very troublesome in France. Perhaps the President of the Republic, Charles de Gaulle, would be toppled; perhaps there would be a coup; perhaps there would be a Marxist revolution.

Charles Wintour, the editor of the London *Evening Standard* thought this was all terrifically exciting. He had the newspaperman's thrill at any momentous event, even one that brought tragedy. (When Robert Kennedy was assassinated in Los Angeles, the news broke at around 8 AM London time, and Charles always said of RFK afterwards – 'He died in our time!' Just perfect for the edition!)

Since I was French-speaking – I had lived for two years in the Paris area, from the ages of eighteen to twenty – Charles thought it a great lark to send me to France: *on a bicycle*. There would be petrol shortages: France would come to a standstill. But I would be *on a bicycle*.

So I went to a bicycle shop in Holborn, hired a bicycle, packed a ruck-sack and set off for Dover. I then cycled from Calais to Paris in about five or six days, reporting the *evenements* in France all along the way. My adventures seem to have been rather closely followed in London, since my bicycle reportage was alluded to elsewhere, and even made an appearance in the trendy Marc Boxer cartoon story called 'The Stringalongs'. In the countryside, there wasn't a huge amount going on, but there was always something to report: I came upon a couple who had sheltered a British air-man during the Second World War, and I was even pursued through a dark copse by a Frenchman in a car at one stage, which the newspaper headline made appear more menacing than it possibly was. Paris was at a standstill when I arrived and the students were indeed revolting all over the streets. One of the first sights I encountered was a group of student-revolutionaries dancing around *La Bourse*, the Parisian stock exchange, which was on fire, exulting: 'The temple of capitalism is burning down!' Not quite yet, it wasn't.

Was this a revolt, a revolution, or the episodic Parisian tendency to *descendre dans la rue* – take to the streets? It was, of course, the latter, but in a particularly heady, almost stylish way. Daniel Cohn-Bendit emerged as the recognised leader of *les soixante-huitards* – the 1968ers – and the word remained in the French lexicon ever after – sometimes disparagingly.

What was it all about? Students trying to overthrow the world they had inherited, yes. Workers in a crisis, maybe. Fabulous wall slogans which I would willingly uphold to this day: *l'imagination au pouvoir; sous les paves – la plage* and *je suis marxiste – tendence Groucho.*

And social historians agree that something indeed happened in 1968: it was a junction year. It was a year when a new generation emerged – perhaps the baby-boom generation of the post-WWII years who had had so many of the benefits, and so few of the sacrifices of any previous generation. There was globalised TV, there was the Pill, and there was a youth culture of rock and roll, which had money. These ingredients were indeed a kind of revolution, but not the kind that necessarily topples presidents from power, rather one that merely subtly begins to change the institutions of state.

When I got to central Paris, I checked in to a small hotel my mother had always used in the Rue Cimarosa, changed out of my biking clothes and dolled myself up a little to join Charles Wintour for drinks at the Ritz. He couldn't keep away from the scenes of radical chic, and had flown over to Paris to see it all for himself. We had champagne and were joined by the television inquisitor Robin Day, who made a pass at me (well, I was a lass of twenty-four – why wouldn't he), but being involved elsewhere, I rebuffed him. Whenever I saw him in later years, he recalled this, always with an air of mock-disappointment and Edwardian gallantry.

Then Charles Wintour said to me – 'you've done a great job on this story, Mary. We're delighted with you. Everyone in London read it. And now . . .' I awaited to see what my reward might be, 'I want you to cycle all the way back.'

And I did just that.

Learning the Language of the Obituary

When the American author Gore Vidal died, the obituaries described him in a number of ways – 'witty and patrician', 'gadfly', 'waspish', and 'acerbic'. Those who had met Mr Vidal said that, actually, he could be awful – dreadfully rude and acidly malicious. He is, after all, the man who said, 'it is not enough to succeed: others must fail', and 'whenever a friend succeeds, a little something in me dies'. He also said, when asked to comment on the case of Roman Polanski's statutory rape of a twelve-year-old girl, 'frankly, I don't give a f***'.

Waspish and acerbic he certainly was: scabrous, malevolent, misanthropic and curmudgeonly could also be applied.

The language of the obituary is often a coded one: I have worked for obituary pages and I grew to learn the code, which is often devised to put a charitable gloss on the character of the deceased. 'He didn't suffer fools gladly', meant 'he was bad-tempered and intolerant'. 'Robust' meant 'tough as nails', and 'combative', 'hopelessly quarrelsome'. 'Loveable rogue' meant 'untrustworthy rascal'; 'he was not always a prudent steward of his assets' meant he was an irredeemable spendthrift.

'She was vivacious and party-loving', meant 'an incorrigible alcoholic'. 'She was popular and vivacious', meant 'a promiscuous alcoholic'. And a 'femme fatale' meant 'she slept with everybody'. 'His personal life was somewhat unusual' meant he had a wife and another family on the side. A colleague of mine – a well-known cartoonist – who died in the arms of his wife, though he had kept a mistress and was known to have patronised call-girls, had this attribute in his obituary: 'his private life defied description'. Of a very flagrant gay man who had many pretty young boyfriends, it was written: 'he was always encouraging to young people'.

Being kind to the dead is right and proper, and a little euphemism never did any harm – anyway, some people deserve all the kindness they receive in memorium. The Irish tend to write much kinder obituaries than the British (or, certainly, than the English), and there are two reasons for this: there is a more deeply-embedded respect for the dead in Irish culture (for which, one day, we, or our families may well be grateful). And being a country of just four million people or thereabouts, there is a dense network of inter-relationships in Ireland. You don't disparage the dead too much because their kinsfolk, and friendly connections, are probably quite numerous.

Yet it is intriguing how words can be used in such a flexible way, sometimes according to the point of view the speaker or the writer wishes to put across: that is, words sometimes say more about the values of the speaker than the character spoken about.

A man may be 'activist' in one political context, a 'campaigner' in another and a 'terrorist' in a third.

If people dislike you they will call you 'intransigent' and 'stubborn'. If they like you they will describe the same traits as 'principled' and 'resolute'.

If you adore a lively child you might call her 'self-willed' or 'spirited', where others might call her 'naughty', 'bold' or 'disobedient'. A man may be admired for showing 'leadership', or he may be disparaged for being a 'bully'.

A woman may be, to one person, 'an articulate conversationalist'; to another a 'garrulous gasbag'. If they like what you are saying they will call you 'committed' and 'passionate'. If they don't like your message, they will call you 'a zealot' and 'a bigot'.

We can see how differently someone like Seán Quinn is viewed, and what different words and language are applied by those who defend him and those who disparage him. For one group of people, he has been the creator of jobs who made some errors of judgement: for others, he is the man who beggared the national exchequer and caused suffering to the poor.

Of a man's behaviour in business it may be said he 'sails close to the wind', by those of a mind to forgive or tolerate what he does: for others he may be 'slippery', 'unethical', a 'swindler', or a 'cheat'. It is all in the intention of the speaker.

Yet some words and expressions have passed into everyday language as common euphemisms, possibly out of kindness, and more probably to avoid legal action and accusations of slander. It can be actionable to call someone a liar, but 'disingenuous' is permissible.

But, trust me, 'disingenuous' usually means 'lying'. 'Dissembling' usually means 'hypocrisy and lying'. 'Ambiguous' – having an intention to deceive. 'Sincere' can mean 'kindly and earnest'; or 'a naïve bloody fool'.

'Challenging' generally now means 'difficult', and quite often means 'delinquent'. 'Challenging behaviour' - can mean 'delinquent and violent'. 'Inscrutable' is a polite word for 'secretive'. It has traditionally been used about the Chinese and Japanese, but the French use it about the English, especially in business and trade.

'Dominant' is what they say about a man, for which the equivalent, in a woman, is 'domineering'. 'Vulnerable' can be a gentle way of saying 'neurotic'. 'Volatile' is another word for 'neurotic' and, actually, 'hysterical'.

'Political' may mean 'clannish'. 'Well-meaning' can be code for 'stupid fool who screws up'. 'Generous' can really mean 'generous', but 'generously endowed' means an over-large bosom. 'Poised and self-assured' in a job reference may indeed mean self-assured and poised: but it might also mean cocky and stuck-up.

'She is an extrovert' can mean 'she is an intolerable show-off'. 'He is introspective' can mean he's a brooding geek who can't communicate with people. And 'serious' can mean 'no sense of humour'.

There are certain euphemisms that I think are terrific. I much prefer to say 'budget', as in 'budget hotel', rather than 'cheap'. 'Economic' sounds better than 'parsimonious'. 'Adversarial' is a nice fancy word for 'argumentative', and a lot more pleasant than 'truculent'. And 'senior citizen' is a lot more cheerful than 'pensioner' or 'elderly person'.

Words are wonderful: they can convey a rich kaleidescope of meanings, knitted together to convey a fascinating subtext. But context matters hugely, and sometimes it really is a question of 'the singer, not the song'.

Life Lessons Journalism Taught Me

Some of the lessons that I learned in my journalistic career only really made sense to me in later life. Perhaps it is always like that. and some of what I learned applied to life as well as to the media.

Some of the lessons imparted to me in my convent school only made sense later in life too: 'A place for everything, and everything in its place.' How I disparaged that tidy bourgeois cast of mind! But now, when I can't find *anything*, I realise there is nothing more useful in the world than that particular adage. Perhaps the most useful lesson of my career in journalism – and again, the penny took some time to drop – was 'preparation is everything.' But it is so true: preparation *is* everything. Anne Sharpley was a great reporter because she prepared. It was a veteran journo from the *Irish Press*, Aidan Hennigan, who instructed me: 'Always do your homework. If you do your homework, nothing can go wrong.' If you're going to interview someone, read biographical background. Carry a notebook and make notes. Keep a clippings file of relevant stories and reports. People do these things electronically now, but the principle is the same. In my heedless youth, I thought I could sometimes 'wing it' – turn up for an interview without doing the preparation work, but I was once, humiliatingly, found out.

I went to interview Eamonn Andrews in the 1970s – he was then a great star of TV and a national celebrity, both in Britain and Ireland – and we were to meet for lunch. We sat down and after the pleasantries, 'Now tell me about your childhood,' I began. 'Why?' asked Eamon. 'Were you too lazy to look up the cuttings?'

It is through painful lessons and humiliating episodes that we learn – and remember.

There was an abiding principle that I did, almost always, fulfill: *always file*. If you have a deadline, you always, always meet it. Drunk or sober, well or ill or caught in a sandstorm in the Gobi desert – file your piece. This training makes a journalist professionally reliable, though possibly negligent about much more important matters (love, marriage, family responsibilities, etc.)

You meet your deadline even when – as has often happened – there isn't much chance of it getting into the paper. In 2000 – rather late in my career – I filed reports from Paris to the *Daily Express* – whither I had been sent on a political story. Not a word appeared in the paper, which was a little galling as I had sacrificed four days amusing myself in Galway to do the job.

But it's like that poem, 'The Listeners' (which Lynn Barber goes to some length to damn in her autobiography, *An Education*. Her elocution-teacher mother loved it, so Lynn thinks it shows ghastly literary taste). There is an important message in the Walter de la Mare narrative, however: 'Tell them I came, and no one answered/That I kept my word, he said.' That is the wider point about 'always file'. You are committed to doing something, so you do it. Even if it never sees the light of day.

Reliability is the greatest reputation a writer can have.

* * *

A newspaper is not a democracy. One man must take the decisions and be responsible for them and as difficult as it could be at times, you had to respect the principle that the editor is always right. Even when he's wrong. It's better to take any decision than no decision. If there's a mistake, there's another paper tomorrow. (This is why journalism is called 'the first draft of history' – it may have to be amended and corrected many times.)

A journalist must go out and about. You cannot do everything from your desk. Every time you go somewhere, you learn something. In times gone by, commissioning editors used to take writers to lunch every now and again. It seldom happens now – indeed writers seldom see their editors, or even know to whom they are filing. Knowledge is thus lost. Working relationships are poorer when there is no face time.

There's nothing like news in a newspaper. Not every newspaper can be a 'paper of record', and many now do not even try to fulfill that remit. But to have something printed, just because it happened, makes for a priceless archive. I only really learned to appreciate how priceless it is when I came to read old newspaper files for the purpose of historical research. The *Irish Catholic* newspaper, for example, covered Parnell's funeral's by noting and printing the names of every single person and organisation who sent floral tributes, and reporting the exact message on each floral display. *That* is the journalism of record. And a great sense of news.

But a news item may be something which has a reader thinking, 'I never knew that' or 'fancy that' when reading it.

You never omit the local angle (or specialist interest). At an editorial conference, Simon Jenkins once gave an example of a Welsh newspaper's 'local angle' *par excellence*: 'Swansea Man marries Swansea Woman in Swansea.' The railway enthusiasts' journal must always see the railway angle: the *Church of England Times* must see the faith angle.

Don't assume knowledge. I was instructed to write 'Mr Harold Wilson, the Prime Minister', because at any given time, eight percent of the readers do not know who the prime minister is. Similarly, don't assume familiarity with a topic just because *you* know about it. Every time Beethoven's Fifth Symphony is played, someone is hearing it for the first time. (Every time a female journalist has a baby, she writes about it as though motherhood has just been invented – we all did.)

Explain acronyms. Maybe everyone knows what the BBC, the UN, and RTÉ stand for, but lesser acronyms often need clarification. If David Cameron, the British Prime Minister, had known 'LOL' meant 'Laugh Out Loud' he wouldn't have used it to mean 'Lots of Love' (to the editor of the *Sun*, always a very powerful person). And if he had been a true Conservative and Unionist, he would have known it also stands for Loyal Orange Lodge.

Shorthand is old-fashioned in the electronic age, but it's still handy and efficient.

You shouldn't have more than two 'knickers' pieces (features about sex) in a newspaper. This is a coded way of saying you must have a balance in a newspaper – never too much of the same thing too often. Readers have different interests.

It was also held as an almost sacred principle that one person's byline hardly ever appeared twice in the same newspaper, and never three times. It made the paper look cheap and like the parish pump gazette. One of the more regrettable developments from the crisis in print newspapers in 2013 is the evident use and overuse of the same writer. In a recent edition of the *Daily Telegraph* review section, one writer had three bylines: it clearly signals the paper is struggling with budgets, which also clearly reduces confidence.

The media always chases the youth market, because young people buy more stuff. Oldies already have most of their stuff purchased. So the youth market will always be important. Also, the media likes to move on and cherish novelty. But successful magazines like *The Oldie* have shown that there is a commercially attractive readership for the over-50s and over-60s, and it's not all stair lifts and cruises. Older readers actually read more, and they are stable in their readership loyalty.

Comment is free but facts are sacred, said C.P. Scott of the *Manchester Guardian*. This was sometimes amended to: comment is free, but facts are expensive.

Anyone can have an opinion, but is it a worthwhile opinion? It took me time to learn that opinions are only worthwhile if based on knowledge or experience, or exceptional insight. Occasionally, an opinion can be engaging just because it's outrageous, or funny, but that is a currency which wears thin if overused.

A columnist should have a voice that regular readers recognise and are beguiled by. As a journalist, Maeve Binchy had that recognisable voice right from the start. With a columnist who has a voice, a light touch on the editorial tiller works best. A commissioning editor should brief a reporter or a feature writer: but a columnist's 'voice' should be trusted. Otherwise, they're not really a columnist.

Ideally, the press should speak 'truth to power', but it often does so selectively. Each newspaper respects a group known as 'protected species' – the people, political party, or interests whom the proprietor wishes to protect. Freedom of the press can only be guaranteed by diversity, not by protocols, much less 'rights', guaranteeing free speech.

The press should speak truth to power, but every journalist needs a friend at court. An enemy at court – a commissioning editor who actively dislikes you or your work – can do damage to any writer's career. Journalism is not cynical, but it works with the grain of human nature, and accepts the doctrine of original sin – man is flawed.

'Remember that the most successful feature we ever ran was "How to dye a sheepskin rug"'. Tim Pat Coogan apprised me of this knowledge when I joined the *Irish Press* as woman's editor. Never underestimate the simple and the practical.

Age is a vital piece of information in reportage. An article about child abuse should always inform us the age of the child in question. The molestation of an eight-year-old is not the same as making a pass at a fifteen-year-old. All exploitation of the young is odious, but the exact age is relevant to the story (since fifteen is for practical purposes the age of consent in the UK, and the contraceptive pill available even earlier, it surely marks a different stage of development from that of a younger child). Names make news. Every mention of a name is news to someone. People purchased copies of the *Cork Examiner* just to read the names of the passengers who boarded the *Titanic* at Queenstown (Cobh). And that was before the disaster. Considering such interest, it was traditionally a firing offence in old Fleet Street to spell a name wrongly. 'Davis' and 'Davies' are not the same person. These things matter to readers.

On names, I personally loathe the new fashion for referring to everyone, men and women indiscriminately, by their surnames only. I blanche when I see myself referred to in print as 'Kenny'. Firstly, it's confusing, and journalism should always try to clarify, not confuse. There are a vast number of people called Kenny (starting with Taoiseach Enda Kenny) and it is an exceptionally common name in Ireland. Kenny is, to confuse matters further, also a first-name, particularly among Australians, being the diminitive of Kenneth. It is woefully impersonal – naturally, because it's just a clan name.

It is generally applied to women as an over-compensatory gesture – the writer is seeking to indicate that they really are egalitarian. Indeed, it is so carefully over-applied to women, that I have seen reports which refer to a woman named by her surname only, and a man named as 'Mr'. ('Smith said she had met Mr Brown only once.') I have also seen reports where a person convicted of a criminal offence is referred to as 'Mr', while a witness is referred to by surname only. Topsy-turvey!

Irish papers are often particularly reluctant to use honorifics: when I have mentioned the former governor of the Bank of England, 'Sir Mervyn King', the 'Sir' has usually been dropped. Irish newspapers also like to lower case 'queen', just to underline the point that the country is not a monarchy. the *Irish Times*, bending over backwards to rebuff its former loyal Southern Unionism, is careful to refer to 'the British Prince Harry', just in case you imagined it was the Norwegian Prince Harry, the Dutch Prince Harry or the Japanese Prince Harry. All these fads and fancies derive from affectations of political correctness rather than sensible rules of journalism.

When the writer is trying to show how cool he or she is, rather than transmitting information that is interesting for the reader, it is a disservice to the trade.

Newspapers need revenue – a point somehow overlooked by those newspapers that put their editions on free websites. Advertising is important, and indeed part of the package of a media service, in most cases.

Never omit mention of love, sex, death, money or royalty in a newspaper feature, where there is an opportunity to allude to them. Especially money. People are very, very interested in money. (And wills).

Always try and get an exact quote as evidence of the substance of a report. Reportage needs evidence.

The most important quality for a journalist is curiosity. What makes people tick? What is the story behind the story? Lord Beaverbrook, the press baron, used to say that 'news is what someone doesn't want you to find out'.

A newspaper should pursue campaigns. But they should be campaigns they can win. A newspaper should never campaign against 'the war on drugs', 'poverty', 'cancer' or 'suicide', because these things will always go on. Pick a specific cause that can actually be won.

If you are bored by what you are writing, the reader will be bored too. If you don't understand what you are writing about, the reader won't understand it either.

A professional writer writes every day.

I was once advised – when struggling with a blank piece of paper in a typewriter, the method of composing then used – 'don't get it right – get it written. Get it right on the re-write.' It is very helpful advice in any writing endeavour. It's getting it down on paper (or on screen) the first time that is the key step. You can then go through as many drafts as you need. The French cultural theorist Roland Barthes said something similar, albeit in a more gnomic formula: 'One cannot write: one can only re-write.'

Most people think they could be journalists, just as most people think they could host a chatshow. Actually, most people can write at least one readable article: many can write several. But journalism is about sustaining the performance, week in, week out. And that's a lot harder. Professional journalists are not particularly appreciative, these days, of politicians equipped with five pensions (thanks to the taxpayer) who decide to take up journalism as a late career – for very little pay, since their five pensions subsidise the writing.

Journalism is not a trusted profession (or trade), and journalists are sometimes referred to as 'hacks'. A caution: a hack is someone who will write anything for money, and will write what they are told to write, like old Soviets following the party line. Not all journalists are hacks in that sense, and most of us have carried on a lifelong battle not to be hacks, but to speak in our own voice. We write for money, but we hope that we don't write just anything for money. (I think I'd rather have the word that Dennis Thatcher brought into currency for the media: 'reptiles'.)

Newspaper proprietors – of which I have known quite a few – are often mad, egomaniacal and eccentric. Sometimes they are wicked and corrupt, like the late Robert Maxwell. Sometimes they are charming and clever, like the adorable Tony O'Reilly or the engaging and intelligent Conrad Black. Yet a man usually buys a newspaper mainly to wield power and exercise influence, and actually, the bonkers press barons who own newspapers for such reasons are often more affable and always more entertaining than the accountants who are only interested in the bottom line.

Keith Waterhouse, a veteran of the journalism trade who went on to be an accomplished novelist and playwright too, once said that a journalist is basically a professional writer, and a professional writer should be able to turn his or her hand to anything. If someone asks for an opera libretto, the professional writer should be able to respond: 'When is the deadline?' (Or, perhaps, in the American wisecrack: 'Do you want it Tuesday, or do you want it good?')

The journalist never writes the headline. But must be aware that some readers blame the journalist for the header.

An editor should lead, inspire, and sometimes intimidate. A successful newspaper is a popular dictatorship.

A deputy editor should be diligent, conscientious, and slave loyally for little recognition. He's the workhorse, like Snowball in *Animal Farm*.

Always read your own newspaper. You must know your market.

The hot news story that you write today will be lining the cat's litter tray tomorrow. Don't flatter yourself that media fame means anything.

Auberon Waugh, son of Evelyn and very successful freelance writer, used to say that every journalist needed 'fuck-off money' – that is, a fund to enable him or her to turn down demeaning or footling assignments. I have never acquired such a fund.

Sometimes the lessons I learned were, I later found out, not the best lessons for life after all – or even for writing. I learned the art of instant reaction: the media is a world where everything is *new, new, new!* And a story will be judged by whether it has a 'new' angle. But sometimes a subject is much improved by waiting, and by reflection, and by playing the long game. The best reportage I have read have been long essays in the *New Yorker*, where a writer has been given time, space and indeed resources to develop a theme thoroughly. A children's writer of my acquaintance, Jane Clarke, has written beautifully about the value of 'composting' an idea. Put an idea away and let it marinade for a while: sometimes something really organic and remarkable develops.

And a real writer, I later learned, does not tell everything. A great writer, like Hemingway, withholds as much as he tells, and allows the reader to do half the imaginative work. Hemingway once wrote a devastating short story, 'Hills Like White Elephants', about abortion, without mentioning the word once.

I learned, alas, to drink in my Fleet Street days, but I also learned how to recover and to appreciate the joy of sobriety. And one of the most useful lessons for life I learned at Alcoholics Anonymous was – 'first things first'. You must focus on priorities to achieve what you seek to achieve. If you are writing something to a deadline, and the house is a mess, the house just has to remain a mess, whatever friends and neighbours will say (and they will).

There will always be a need for reportage, for knowledgeable and well-researched comment, and also for entertainment in the media. But I would not advise any young person today to choose the print media as a career. 'We are experiencing,' a veteran editor remarked to me, 'the dissolution of the monasteries.' That is a useful parallel: as print overtook monks' manuscripts – bringing about a social and cultural revolution – so electronic media is overtaking print. Scoops and stories now break on Twitter and Facebook before there is a chance to get into print. There will always be print, but it will be greatly diminished, and it will be difficult for younger generations to make a living as a print journalist. The days of 'To hire of camel - £500' expenses are well and truly over for journalists. Go into the law, young lady: lawyers always make money!

Talking about Uganda

George Orwell once said that the only autobiography worthy of trust is one that reveals something disgraceful about the writer. This collection is not an autobiography, but a series of selective memoirs; yet I might address the above just the same.

When I was twenty-seven years of age, I got very plastered indeed one night after receiving some pessimistic medical news. I had had a pain in my hip for some time, and my GP had taken me to a particularly doleful surgeon who gave me a bad prognosis: he said I would always be lame, and I would never be able to carry a pregnancy. (This turned out to be an absurdly over-pessimistic prognosis, but my late GP, Gerry Slattery, did point out afterwards that the surgeon was a South African Communist, with a melancholy cast of mind.)

However, after this medical ordeal, I drank myself silly, and a very stupid episode occurred at a friend's party later that evening whose details, thankfully, I can scarcely remember. But there was a rather shameful snogging session with an intelligent African judge, and when we were surprised by other guests, I apparently said we were only 'talking about Uganda' (I had recently reported from Kampala). The lawyer himself, bless him, only had one leg (though I noticed nothing of that at the time, after the twelve gin and tonics, five glasses of wine and a large armagnac). This was all considered killingly funny and taken up by the satirical magazine *Private Eye* with gusto: the poet James Fenton thought it so utterly hilarious that he managed to enter the phrase in a reference dictionary of slang. For more than forty years, now, *Private Eye* has thought it side-splittingly droll to refer to dubious sexual encounters as 'talking about Uganda'.

Satirical magazines should make heartless fun of those in power, especially political power. But gagging with laughter over the drunken frolics of a freelance journalist with no access to power, influence or money is scarcely Swiftian humour. Especially when the editor of *Private Eye*, nowadays, is himself a figure of much celebrity, influence and considerable wealth – married to a best-selling novelist. The joke about 'talking about Uganda' is an interesting example of the big people satirising the little people, rather than the other way about.

It also became distinctly less comical when it transpired that the unfortunate African lawyer – a man of courageous principles in his professional life - was subsequently murdered by Idi Amin, and his mutilated body was discovered at the bottom of Lake Victoria. Very unfunny indeed.

To be sure, if we make fools of ourselves we have to face the consequences, and the humiliation that disclosure can bring. I thought myself mightily clever for revealing poor George Brown's flaws – and I have found out that in life, you do, often, get repaid in your own coin. Heigh-ho: we reap as we sow – just as the nuns warned us!

Part Two
My Part in Famous Lives

I Made the President's Match

It was graceful of President Michael D. Higgins to mention, in a number of media interviews, that he had first met his wife, Sabina, at a party in my Dublin flat in 1969.

My previously cloudy recollection of that soirée – you know what they say about the 1960s: if you can remember what happened, you weren't there – was indeed revived. Somewhat. It was one of those entertaining but chaotic evenings (I would start cooking for a party, in my Dublin flat, at 6.30 PM when guests were expected at 7 PM) from which Mr Ulick O'Connor, the *litterateur*, stormed out, as he felt (unreasonably) that some-one had insulted him: he was given to that kind of gesture, and some others, more combative and pugilistic. The air was pleasantly thick with talk, arguments, song and story.

In retrospect, a significant element of the gathering turned out to be that Michael D. – an admired young left-wing academic at the time – was to encounter Sabina Coyne, who had been brought along to the gathering by my late sister.

Sabina and my sister Ursula were both enthusiastic students of the drama, as taught by Deirdre O'Connell of the Focus Theatre. Deirdre O'Connell was a drama teacher of some renown in Dublin: she took theatre with high-minded seriousness, usually wore black, and had, I believe, stud-ied 'the Method' school of acting with Lee Strasbourg in New York (where Marlon Brando and Marilyn Monroe also learned the thespian art). My sis-ter worshipped Deirdre O'Connell for her High Art approach to drama; so different from the usual Dublin quick-to-mock attitude to everything.

My sister Ursula thought Sabina – a lively and vivacious girl – was won-derful, and full of theatrical promise. And serendipity struck when Sabina and Michael D. met each other on that occasion, and it was a meeting of true minds and hearts. I believe the president recalls my effecting the actual introductions – thus being the agency of the match – and I hope I was well-mannered enough to do so nicely. A veil of alcoholic mist hangs over many of the events of my youth – in some cases, fortunately, in this case, regrettably. In any case, the *coup de foudre* was struck between Sabina and Michael D., and in the fullness of time, marriage and four children followed. And I have earned my small place as a footnote in history in having made the match of the 9th Uachtarán na hÉireann, and I only wish my sister Ursula had lived to see the presidential elevation. For anyone seeking love or romance, the advice must be – attend every party that comes your way, for you never know what magic might occur.

I would at that time have shared Michael D.'s left-wing vision of politics – I seem to remember I had the regulation poster of Che Guevara on the walls (and him a Galway man too – well, his name being Lynch, a forebear hailing from Galway). Over the years, I'd have waxed critical of some of our president's political values – his enthusiasm for Sandanista socialism and the Palestinians claims – and I daresay he'd have had scant respect for some of mine – my sometime enthusiasm for Margaret Thatcher and my assertion that we must stand by the Jews, and thus Israel.

Yet I believe that 'right-wing' and 'left-wing' are too simplistic and crude as definitions nowadays: most people have opinions that encompass both. Many 'conservatives' are 'social liberals' (they are liberal on issues like gay marriage and abortion); many liberals are not at all liberal when it comes to some areas of individual choice – they believe that all-male clubs should be disallowed and that "hate speech" should be banned – a point of view, certainly, but it's hardly 'liberal'. Some Leftists remain 'socially conservative' on some issues: they may be against euthanasia and, particularly since Islamic culture became more visible in Europe (and a factor in voting), they can be more careful about not offending traditional religious sensibilities. On immigration, the rich, and otherwise, conservatives are often 'liberal', since immigration provides staff at a lower price, while the white working class are understandably more resentful. It is all much more muddled up than it used to be (and some of us change our minds regularly, anyway).

The real difference is not between those historic divisions between left and right, as I see it, but between those who live by their labour – manual, professional or intellectual – and those who enjoy security of tenure, a guaranteed monthly cheque, paid holidays and safe pensions. And that is where my life experience would be rather different from that of President Higgins.

I think it can be argued that those of us out here in the market-place of capitalism are the true 'working class'. We live by the sweat of our brows, without any subsidy from the taxpayer. If we don't work, we don't eat. For the freelance worker, there are no paid holidays and no security of tenure and if you're too unwell to work, you don't earn revenue (so you are seldom too unwell to work). Every penny earned depends on your ability to sell your labour: that is the definition of working class – those who sell their labour. More than once, I have heard old journos compared to old harlots: still plying their trade up and down the street, if raddled in their looks, at least practised in their experience, and knowledgeable about what the punter wants – 'I may not be the prettiest, gov, but I know a trick or two.'

That is where the divergence would occur between President Higgins's experience and mine, I'd suggest. He has been an academic, a scholar, a senator, an elected politician and a government minister before attaining the office of the presidency in November 2011 (and by far the most worthy candidate in that election, too). All these posts are in the public sector and supported by the taxpayer. I describe: I do not complain or disparage. Ireland is honoured to have a poet as the head of state, and while he has led a working life more sheltered than I, hardship and penury is not unknown to his experience, for his childhood was one of many difficulties – his parents struggling to run a business in the hard times of the 1930s, and being obliged to send their sons to an aunt's farm in County Limerick.

Thus, in his mission of inclusiveness, I hope he will always think to include those of us of that working class who must earn our bread through capitalism: unfair as capitalism often is, it is the only system that can, literally, produce the goods.

Without the wheels of commerce – as Fernand Braudel has shown in his history of civilisation – there would be no arts, no culture, no film industry, no books. The brilliance of Dutch painting was made possible by the rapacity of Dutch merchants in the East Indies; neither the Renaissance nor the Enlightenment would have happened without the risks – and the greed – of the merchant princes who sallied forth to plunder for wealth. Venice would never have been the hub of trade and commerce which brought every globalised product to Europe without men who took risks for profits.

Actually, I share Michael D.'s dislike of the 'loadsamoney' braggadoccio of recent times – sometimes exemplified by the extravagance and speculation seen during the period of Irish history known as the era of the Celtic Tiger, and subsequently seen in the odious conduct of the bankers. Greed is a cardinal sin, but man is a fallen creature: I don't admire the self-regarding vanity seen on the faces of the seventeenth century Dutch merchants whose fine portraits adorn the Rijksmuseum in Amsterdam either, but without the energy that drives these periods of greed, there is no development. I witnessed the end of the Soviet Empire. There was nothing in the shops.

At the time Michael D. came to my soirée, I'd have admired figures like Gramsci or Leon Trotsky – my favourite book at that time was *To the Finland Station*, Edmund Wilson's exciting text, written in 1940, on the development of socialist ideas. Today my heroes are more prosaic (and my reading less political): I admire entrepreneurs who start small businesses, with vision, industry and inspiration, battling through bureaucratic regulations about health and safety, employment law and working time EU directives. I see a man setting up a restaurant, into which he has sunk all his savings, gutting the premises and painting it all himself, and I think – what courage, to do that. These valiant souls achieve something original, give employment to others, and are significant cogs in those wheels of commerce which make civilisation possible.

I don't expect Michael D. to have forsaken Hugo Chavez and his legacy – he has a strong attachment to Latin American socialism, which emerges quite lyrically in his poetry. It must sometimes be something of a struggle for Michael D. – who has been a politician most of his working life – to remain as politically neutral, and uncontroversial, as an Irish head of state is expected to be, being above politics. But he is a constitutional expert; he knows the limitations of the office of the presidency, yet he knows too, that the office can be used inspirationally or elastically.

He has spoken of his desire to be a force for unity and inclusiveness, underlining the traditions in Irish life of 'sharing' – as in the harvesting tradition of *Meitheal*. Michael D. feels that capitalism has too sharply stressed the individualistic values of money-making and we need to return to a more co-operative social approach. Well, if we ever meet again on another occasion, perhaps we can continue that conversation. And I'll certainly congratulate both the president and his wife, Sabina – who has been an entrancing consort, full of personality – for finding each other that merry night *chez moi* in 1969.

Mary Robinson was in My Feminists' Consciousness-raising Group

Yes, shamefully, I did immediately look myself up in the index when Mary Robinson published her autobiography, *Everybody Matters*, in 2012, since I had known Mary Robinson (née Bourke) when we were both young feminists in Dublin in 1970 and I was one of the authors of the Irish Women's Liberation's blueprint, *Chains or Change*.

Indeed, Mary sat in my Dublin flat sharing 'conscious-raising' sessions, and I published one of the first political interviews with her in the *Irish Press* in April 1970, which is a source for previous biographies, notably Michael O'Sullivan's *Mary Robinson:The Life and Times of an Irish Liberal*. She was then a young Senator in Seanad Éireann, full of energy and anxious to do more with her life than hang around what was then a rather sleepy version of the Irish upper house. She called the Seanad 'obsolete, expensive, [a] cumbersome mechanism, purely drafting government legislation'. She told me that she felt like 'walking up and down outside the parliamentary buildings on Kildare Street with a placard which read "I am Under-Employed"', a sentiment which Michael O'Sullivan described as 'an almost theatrical performance playing to the gallery'.

I was introduced to Mary by the poet Eavan Boland, who I used to meet every Saturday morning at the coffee-shop at Brown Thomas. Eavan was – and no doubt, still is – clever, funny, highly-strung, and at that time, personally conventional. Eavan thought me bold and naughty and outrageous – all perfectly fair judgements – and I think she rather enjoyed the idea that I was being bold and naughty and outrageous so that she didn't have to be. This is a role I have often played in the lives of more naturally virtuous people.

Mary Bourke was (and is) one of Eavan's closest friends, and they were similar in many respects: both upper-middle-class schoolgirls who had been star pupils, prefects and head girls at Ireland's elite convent, Mount Anville. Eavan's father was Frederick Boland, the distinguished Irish diplomat; her mother was a renowned portrait painter, Frances Kelly. Mary's family were Catholic gentry – her parents were doctors, and she had a clatter of relations who had served the Crown before Irish independence: she could also trace her family back to Charlemagne.

In retrospect it seems nearly inevitable that she would become president of Ireland, then graduating to being one of the world's great panjandrums, UN High Commissioner for Human Rights, with forty-nine honorary doctorates from universities all over the globe and honours from half a dozen countries, including the Presidential Medal of Freedom bestowed by President Obama. There is almost no international honour or award which, by 2012, Mary Robinson had not attained.

I always thought Mary Robinson courageous, principled and admirable: she took decisions in her life based on what she thought was right. Some of that courage and that sense of principle are, I think, derived both from her class and her family background; she was the only girl in a family of boys, and cherished as such, from the start. She was given every educational advantage in life, and it was that psychological parental support which spurred her on to her many achievements. Nothing is as supportive of a successful life as a stable family background.

If Mary was admirable and courageous she was also, even as a young woman, a little on the humourless side, and somewhat daunting. And always high-minded: she reveals in her memoir that when it was arranged that she should appear in *Hello!* magazine (as a presidential candidate) that she had never heard of the publication, let alone devoured it for gossip about Princess Diana, like ordinary mortals. It is as if she has always lived in a milieu above ordinary mortals – including those she seeks to help, from her position of responsibility. Even as a law student at Trinity College Dublin, she had her own house in Westland Row, with her own maid, and she was known to open the hall door wearing ballgown gloves.

Our feminists' meetings – this was in the formation of the Irish Women's Liberation Movement in 1970 – were lively, informal, talkative, sometimes a little ragged. When Mary attended, she always brought a sense of order and decorum to the proceedings. She had convictions, but I think some of us were a little in awe of her dignity and decorum. We would not have got drunk in her presence, when otherwise we often would.

From an early age, Mary was aware of her privileges and like many an anguished Guardianista, it is the guilt about such privilege which drives her to embrace progressive causes, and care for the excluded – for example, the 'travelling people' (we formerly called them tinkers) and the gay community that she invited to the presidential mansion, though not, of course, at the same time.

Two of her aunts were nuns, and at seventeen she thought of entering the convent herself. In some respects, Mary is a little like the best kind of nun: serious-minded, ordered, conscientious, determined to do good, concerned about the world's poor, especially in Africa and other missionary locations, and confident in her own values. Although married (to Nick Robinson) with three children and now four grandchildren, she is as reserved as a nun about sexual matters, and in her writings, it is implied that she retained her virginity until she met her husband.

Mary did everything right, just around the same time as I did everything wrong. She never did anything to excess: even living in Paris as a young woman, to enjoy the odd glass of wine counted as a daring experience. (She was at a finishing school in France just about the same time as I was an au pair – read, skivvy – to a family with seven children.)

Yet moral courage she has in abundance. She disdained to join our feminist stunt involving the 'condom train' travelling from Belfast to Dublin (though in her memoir, she gets the detail slightly wrong: the stunt wasn't 'in defiance of the customs officers', who were either pink with embarrassment or winking in jovial compliance – it was in defiance of an antiquated 1935 law). She supported Mairin de Burca's cause to restore women to jury service (actually, women had served on juries in the early years of the Free State, but they had so often asked to be excused from serving that the Justice Minister, Kevin O'Higgins, decided in 1927 that it was simpler not to call women at all.)

Mary fought through the courts, and by using the constitution, to dismantle these archaic statutes and took up the cause, too, of decriminalising homosexuality. She upset her parents – who were orthodox Catholics of their time – with her actions, and learned thereby that you must sometimes pay a price for a principle. But she didn't flinch from acting according to these principles.

Mary is a great believer in the law as a political force: she interpreted the Irish constitution both imaginatively, and as a lawyer, and I once heard her give a lecture about Daniel O'Connell as a lawyer – at my club in London, the Reform, of which O'Connell had been a founding member – and what a great leap forward it was when he advanced the cause of the Irish nation through the law, rather than through agitation or violence.

I thoroughly applauded and thoroughly agreed – although I was aching with hunger at the time of this lecture, as she insisted on speaking before dinner, so as not to ruin her own meal with pre-speech anxiety. Yet lawyers sometimes have a *déformation professionelle* about the law: it is vital, but it isn't everything. As Edmund Burke knew, human society is also a matter of custom, practice, community pressures, intuition, family values, and even, occasionally, the wisdom of turning a blind eye to the letter of the law. It is not good for a society to have too many lawyers: it always means more litigation, more expensive court cases, and above all, more compensation to be paid, with the mentality of the compo culture that follows. Great emphasis on what is legal or illegal may occlude what is decent, what is honourable, what is good practice, or even what is mannerly. ('Hate speech' is horribly unkind, but should that be a matter for the law? Lawyers think so.)

Mary quit her post as president of Ireland in 1997, twelve weeks before the end of her term, which was an error of judgement that is still resented by some in Ireland. She had the greatest privilege an Irish citizen can have, that of being elected Uachtarán na hÉireann, and she abridged the office so as to be a bureaucrat of the United Nations, in the United States. Subsequently, she expressed regret for her haste and noted a coolness towards her even in her home county.

But I wondered if that was partly the same impatience that she expressed to me in that 1970 interview, when she felt the need to press on, press on. And so she did: proceeding to her many illustrious globalised posts, and becoming one of the universal band of the Great and Good, a leading member of The Elders, and active in her Ethical Globalisation Initiative, whose purpose is to introduce ethical guidelines to globalised activity, perhaps filling the gap left by the decline of traditional religion.

As it happens, I do not appear in the index of Mrs Robinson's memoir, which may be for the best, since my cast of mind is sometimes more critical than adulatory – maybe that's a fancy way of saying 'chippy'. I was never close to Mary Robinson – bad girls are seldom best friends with head girls – though our relations were cordial, and I certainly admire her. Though I would make one criticism, which is one that arises from other voices from time to time: there is no mention of money in her discourses, and she has never disclosed how much she has earned from the taxpayer, Irish and global, throughout her distinguished career, and now via the accretion of pensions. Besides her United Nations emoluments, she must qualify for three Irish pensions, as former president and former senator, and former professor of law at Trinity College Dublin; as well as an entitlement to many travel expenses.

Perhaps this curiosity, on my part, also has a personal provenance: I once shared a taxi with Mary Robinson between Heathrow Airport and central London – we were both, I think, arriving from separate missions in Brussels, and if my memory serves me right, I paid for the fare, although working journalists are seldom as well remunerated as gilded international lawyers.

I was Edna O'Brien's Secretary

I can't remember how I got the job of doing secretarial work for Edna O'Brien in the early 1960s. I think I encountered her at some Irish literary occasion and she said she had need of a typist. I certainly didn't deserve the job, as I was a hopelessly disorganised secretary. But Edna was kind, and she must have hired me out of kindness.

As an employer she was easy and indulgent. She fed me cake and Burgundy, which I thought wonderful and terribly sophisticated.

I would go to her London home at Deodar Road in Putney, just over the river from Fulham. Edna was in her thirties then, beautiful and sought-after, but she had a vague, otherworldly air, sylphlike and whisperey. Her clothes, from the designer Thea Porter – who specialised in a high-class gypsy look – enhanced her persona.

I was supposed to deal with her letters, but my recollection is that we didn't get through too many. There was always so much else going on. She was a fond mother to her sons, Sasha and Carlo, but she was also a divorced woman on her own, and, I think, looking for love.

One day she lamented there were no available men in London. Anyone decent was immediately snapped up. 'There must be some, Edna,' I said. 'What about widowers?' I added brightly.

'By God, you'd have to grab them on the way back from the funeral!' she replied sardonically.

I thought Edna had everything – talent, looks, children, a home, and lots of sparkling friends, but I could sense that she had this predilection for loneliness. 'Oh, Mary, age – think of it! And death! It's terrifying!'

There was a needy vulnerability about her, and yet a contradiction too; a steely purposefulness in her work, combined with a fragility in relationships.

Her brand of Irishness was beguiling. She had retained that 'colleen bawn' Irish country charm, and yet she was metropolitan and belonged as much to Chelsea as to County Clare.

She radiated sex-appeal, but her allure seemed part of a style which younger feminists were beginning to reject. Edna wanted to be in love and to be loved, and maybe even protected, by a man. While the rising feminist generation were coining phrases like 'a woman needs a man like a fish needs a bicycle', and were declaring that love and sex could only be on equal terms and without dependency. Feminine softness was out: bold affirmation of sexuality was in.

But it was Edna who lasted the course, and it will be Edna who will be remembered, both as artist and as eternal woman.

* * *

I most recently saw Edna at a celebratory dinner at the Irish Embassy in London. At eighty-two, she remained as glamorous and as striking as she appears in those renowned photographs of her salad days.

She said she would never write a memoir, since her life is in her work, but in the end, wiser counsels prevailed: a writer must leave a record and an archive, and she published *Country Girl* in 2012. It is a work full of the O'Brien enchantments, the lushness about nature, the delicate balance of rapture and rupture in recapturing the experience of love, the feminine eye for dress, the true ear for a story, the sharpness of specific recollections.

Some of the stories Edna recounts in her retrospective are familiar, since they already appear in her fiction. There is a passage about her ardent, adolescent experience of falling in love with a nun – 'in a manner no different, no less rapturous, from the successive loves which I would conceive for men down the years.' She has written about this episode in a short story but it loses none of its clarity and poignancy in the retelling.

The classic themes of her early novels – the break with her parents over a forbidden love affair – re-emerge as autobiography, but now with a slightly different sheen. In the novel *The Country Girls,* the family can be read as brutal, rough peasants standing in the way of a daughter's right to liberty, but more subtly, in retrospect, we can see that her parents naively trying to protect the young Edna from a disastrous marriage, as indeed it turned out to be. Ernest Gébler, her husband, was more verbally abusive than any Irish censor – comparing Edna, ludicrously, with Krafft-Ebing, of the weird sexual fetishisms. A chilling account of a court case in which she finally wins custody of her sons is as dramatic as anything in her fiction.

In London, she came to be part of a high-octane celebrity scene: she knew Paul McCartney, Lord Snowdon, Richard Burton, R.D. Laing (with whom she experimented with LSD), Sean Connery, Maggie Smith – and then Beckett, Marguerite Duras, Pinter, the Oliviers, and Marlon Brando, with whom she passed a chaste night, and Robert Mitchem, with whom she passed a carnal one. She had a house in Carlyle Square which was often filled with great names, from Harold Wilson to Ingrid Bergman. She sold that house at not a good time in the real estate market, mainly, I think, to help out her children, and remembers it with nostalgia and perhaps yearning – an Edna O'Brien trope.

Edna, in her prime, led a fabulous life in London and New York (where she knew Al Pacino, Norman Mailer and had a rewarding friendship, vividly evoked, with Jacqueline Kennedy Onassis). Yet she was always approachable and almost humble; she never had her head turned by celebrity because she is fundamentally a hard-working artist, who takes her cue from the obsessive dedication of James Joyce, and thus knows that while celebrity life can be gratifying, it is ephemeral, and you do not lose sight of the work.

I saw her on and off throughout the 1970s. She sweetly came to parties that Marjorie Wallace and I gave in our London flat, and occasionally had me to dinner. She was once very much in love with a man I knew (quite platonically) and she needed to talk about him. He was a man of many amours and not inclined to be faithfully responsive even to such a beguiling woman as Edna, then in her later forties.

Rightly, Edna O'Brien is now seen as an Irish national treasure, and while the Irish state has no honours to bestow, she is given much honour in general. It is oft repeated that Edna's early books were banned by the Irish Catholic church: if so, they were, by some form of Irish ambiguity also easily available, and even on display, as I recall, on the shelves of the Eblana bookshop then on Grafton Street (and run by the celebrated Irish showjumper, Iris Kellett). In her memoir, Edna discloses that it was Charles J. Haughey, then Irish minister for justice who denounced Edna's first novel as 'filth', while it was a priest, Father Peter Connolly, who was Edna's literary champion and who defended her against a raft of womenfolk who regarded her as a hussy for writing about a young girl who makes away with a married man.

Edna is a woman of endurance, and a person of kindness, as well as a very great artist, and if I hadn't been so foolish as to get a job in journalism at the end of my stint as her secretary, I would have been privileged to serve her for life.

I hired Delia Smith

The year was 1972, and I was Features Editor of the *London Evening Standard* in old Fleet Street. Sadly, the previous cookery writer employed by the newspaper was beginning to show signs of senility, forgetting to put the onions in an onion quiche and the like.

In my usual irresponsible way, I thought this was rather funny and a good test of how closely the readers were following the daily recipes. But the word went out from on high: a new cookery writer had to be found.

Delia's approach to that job interview, which I conducted, was impressive. Indeed, it should probably be included in some kind of school-leaver's advice book on 'How to Succeed at a Job Interview'. She turned up looking fresh and clean and bright. Her clothes were pleasant but not provocative: her manner was friendly and outgoing but somehow implying, in the subtlest possible way, respect. She only had to sit down opposite you before you knew she would be completely and utterly reliable, never give any trouble, never omit the onions from the onion quiche, never be moody, difficult, drunk, pre-menstrual, or even ill. She would not – as, tragically, the home decorator writer had just done – slit her wrists after being abandoned by a cruel lover. (The suicide was successful, much to the vexation of the chief sub-editor, who was left with a hole in his page.)

Delia would not, as one of the ace women reporters had done, exclaim angrily, to a listening newsroom – 'where the hell is the number of that bloody Harley Street abortionist? I need his services again, dammit!' She would not cause tears at the editorial conference over a stormy love affair with the deputy editor. She would not, like the drama critic, develop a problem with slow horses and large gambling debts. She would not, like another star writer on the staff, be found holidaying in Thailand with underage boys. She would not join the Maoist party, as the editor's secretary had done, and be seen marching to Trafalgar Square holding up the Little Red Book and calling for the extermination of bourgeois intellectuals.

In a notoriously badly-behaved profession, Delia just radiated that head-girl sense and shining integrity. And yet, interestingly, Delia did not have a single academic accolade: she had left school at sixteen without passing any exams. But she had soon applied herself to the University of Life. She had gone out into the world and got herself some genuine work experience. She had gravitated towards cooking having done a variety of other jobs, and in a London restaurant, she had started at the bottom, as humble kitchen porter. She was then quite fortunate in doing a stint of training under Clement Freud, cook, parliamentarian (grandson of Sigmund, brother of Lucian), who taught her much about food.

From then on, she taught herself. She worked and watched and improved. She devoured recipe books in libraries and developed a method of writing recipes which put a premium on clarity.

Delia had 'eagerness' and 'diligence' written all over her. Anyone would have hired her, I just happened to be the one sitting in the editorial chair at the time.

She was an instant and continuing success at the newspaper, and went on to produce her own books and television series. At the last count, she had sold some 18 million cookbooks, and her fans always say of Delia, 'her recipes *work*.' She became very rich indeed. Married (to Michael Wynn Jones), and childless (not by choice), Delia was involved with her Norfolk community and a philanthropist to her football team, Norwich City. She retained her Catholic faith, in a devotional, private way, rather than as a blaring public statement. She wrote a helpful spiritual book which combined food and spirituality, *A Journey into God*.

In the communications industry – of which cooking is now very much a part – you may have a time when you are 'hot', and then, gradually, or suddenly, someone else is 'hot' and your time of warmth in the sun is over, as is the natural course of things. If you are lucky, you then become a veteran of the business and if you live long enough you may become a 'national treasure'.

Delia's sensible and helpful persona was somewhat overtaken by the flashier celebrity cooks, and Nigella Lawson's Cleopatra-like beauty came – for a time – to occlude all other female cooks, at least on British television. Delia went on being a respected name in cooking – she turned seventy in 2012 – and her fan base remained solid, but like many oldies she eventually succumbed to the temptation of lamenting the way the world was going, and came to disparage the ultra-cult of the 'celebrity cook'. It had, she said, become excessive, and too dependent on gimmicks. Although she had benefited from her own fame, the obsession with food and cooking on television, by the second decade of the twenty-first century, had got to a point almost of decadence. Were the Cromwellites entirely wrong to denounce those who 'make a god out of their belly'? Anything disproportionate becomes *de trop*.

Delia was lucky in her time – she was on the cusp of that wave when food was rediscovered as one of the domestic arts. But if she was lucky, she was also deserving of her success: her winning sincerity, unaffected friendliness and appetite for diligent application made Delia Smith a household name, and her personality remains unchanged since the day she sat before me as a job applicant, radiating reliability.

I interviewed Marlene Dietrich . . .

It was 1966 and I was a young reporter on the *Evening Standard*'s 'Londoner's Diary'. La Dietrich was appearing at the Savoy and I was selected to go and interview the lady, who was one of my teenage idols. (I was a weird, retro teenager with no interest in rock 'n' roll, but obsessed by movies and chansons of the 1930s. A defining moment of my adolescence was seeing Dietrich in *Shanghai Express*, when the jodhpur-clad Clive Brooks asks her, as an old flame, if she ever married: 'It took more than one man to change my name to Shanghai Lil', she replies, smokily. I practised that in the mirror afterwards for days.)

But perhaps one should never meet one's idols. Dietrich was at the time of life where she really was beginning to feel her age – she concealed her age carefully but she was born in 1901 – however skilfully she had been able to disguise it until then. She was fatigued and world-weary. All she really said – and she said it over and over again: 'All my friends are dead. Hemingway is dead. Cocteau is dead. Gary Cooper is dead.' I wrote down what she said, but I felt terribly disillusioned somehow.

I was too young to appreciate her feelings properly, which were perhaps all the more melancholy for a great star facing old age. Old stars find old age difficult: losing beauty and desirability is humiliating. Subsequently, I encountered Vivien Leigh at a reception in Mayfair. She was reasonably well-preserved but her eyes carried an expression of rueful sadness, a sighing alienation. My sister Ursula, working for the BBC in New York, had dealings with an elderly Ginger Rogers, who told her smartly: 'Old age is not for sissies.' Ursula repeated that herself in her sixties.

Now, I often think of Dietrich's words – 'All my friends are dead', as many of my friends are indeed dead. But I try to learn from what she said.

When your friends die, a tranche of your life and your shared experiences dissolves. Every year you live past sixty-five, you should make at least one new friend, annually.

. . . and Judy Garland . . .

It was January 1969 when I was sent to interview Judy Garland, who was due to perform at the *Talk of the Town*. The deal was that I should first watch the show, and then go backstage to talk to the star. The show was a catastrophe. Three-quarters of an hour after she was due to appear on stage, there was still no sign of Miss Garland. Her fans were normally fanatically loyal to her, but now they were jeering, cat-calling, stomping and whistling in derision. Finally, after midnight Judy Garland tottered onto the stage. But what ensued was painful to watch. She couldn't even warble 'Over the Rainbow'. A Croydon housewife was so infuriated that she climbed up on the stage and sang herself. Everyone cheered. Judy was booed off.

Later I was escorted backstage by a nervous agent. We went into her dressing room, where we saw her friend Johnny Ray (who had also tried to help the situation by performing himself) and Judy's much younger husband, Mickey Deans. The physician who accompanied her everywhere was also present.

Judy Garland was hiding behind a curtain covering the washbasin, and she peeped out, like a naughty child. She gave an unsteady grin and then emerged, boyish and frail, in a spangled trouser suit. She shook my hand and just said: 'Look, dear, I couldn't face an interview tonight. I'm being hounded by lawyers and doctors and every goddam thing. Tomorrow – come back tomorrow.' Her face looked ravaged but she had nice, desperate eyes; there was something hugely vulnerable about her. You felt she had been torn apart by life.

Impulsively, she took up a little bunch of flowers, expensively set and wired, and thrust them into my hand, as if in compensation. 'Here, have these,' she said.

I returned to the *Talk of the Town* the next night and the next and the next. Her performances varied enormously: sometimes she showed the old flash of her great vocal genius. But she never felt up to doing the arranged interview. And honestly, she wasn't.

She died less than six months later, aged forty-six.

. . .and Natalie Wood . . .

I was sent to meet Natalie Wood at the Dorchester Hotel. She was tiny, and wore the most exquisite leopardskin (or possibly ocelot) fur coat I have ever seen. It was not just the perfection of the animal skin that was striking, it was the *cut*. And the way it was so flawlessly lined. She was pretty but she had very little to say: she liked her Russian heritage – her original name had been Natasha.

All that I really remember was the coat.

. . . and Estée Lauder . . .

Estée Lauder received me in her New York office. I thought her down-to-earth and professional. To her, I must have been an obscure Irish journalist – she did the interview for the *Irish Press* – but her attitude was that it was part of her job to give her time, courteously, to those who sought her out. She was aware that she was her own brand, but had no grand cosmetics-queen attitudes. She was a sensible Jewish grandmother whose own skin looked pretty good.

Her main advice to me (which I have surely followed) was that 'after forty, a woman has to choose between her face and her figure. Never diet too much, or your face will grow haggard. And always eat at least a small pat of butter each day. Butter is essential for the body's oils.'

... and Gloria Steinem ...

In the 1960s and 1970s, Gloria Steinem was, even to the most hostile critic of feminism, the most charming and engaging of women's liberation avatars. She had been pretty enough to work as a Bunny Girl at one of Hugh Hefner's loathsome Playboy clubs – she undertook the job only to expose the way women were regarded as objects at the disposal of Hefner's clients. She wrote well, and we had lunch at a restaurant in Greenwich Village. She had a most captivating laugh – very engaging and tinkley – and certainly combined feminism with feminity. Then in her thirties, she glowed, and was always generous about encouraging other women. She was also witty: when speaking about marriage she said 'I can't mate in captivity'. Actually, she chose not to mate at all until she was in her sixties.

In later life, I interviewed her again, in London, but this time the chemistry was not so harmonious. I had children by then and she was emphatic about choosing not to have children. The care of old people moved her more than the charm of young children. She was glad she had terminated a pregnancy. Later on again, I noticed that she became obsessive about 'reproductive control', in global terms, and she grew very thin indeed, seeming like one of those old-time American schoolmarms who lay down the law with a lemony kind of austerity. But she retained the tinkley laugh.

... and Marlon Brando and Gregory Peck ...

Two very contrasting characters: I got to meet Brando when he was doing a movie with Charlie Chaplin and Sophia Loren called *The Countess from Hong Kong*. It was a mediocre film and there was a lot of dissatisfaction on the set, but Chaplin was directing and his name and status drew respect. I only got to see Brando because the publicity agent handling the movie – a lovely Jewish New Yorker who had had to leave the US because of his 'Red' leanings, during the McCarthy era ('honey, we were in the same Communist cell' were words I heard in this milieu) – took a fancy to me. Yes, young women in mini-skirts certainly did use whatever feminine or sexual power at their command – always have and always will.

I couldn't get anything much out of Brando. He was perfectly cordial, but essentially, he didn't have a lot to say. He talked a bit about the plight of the Native American people, and that was it. And why should he have anything much to say? Why should we expect actors to be original thinkers or conversationalists? It's not their job. Their job is to get into the character that they are playing and bring that character to life. Perhaps the greater the actor, the less he may have to say about anything in particular.

Gregory Peck was not a great actor, but he was a great screen star, and a very nice man. I met him in the 1980s, and interviewed him for the *Irish Independent*. I looked absolutely ghastly as I had a mighty hangover, and hadn't had time to do any repair work on my face. But he couldn't have been more thoughtful, generous with his time, and indeed, interesting. He spoke a lot about his mother's career, and how she had been, in the early years of the twentieth century, a travelling saleswoman for ladies' lingerie. She was quite a pioneer, he felt. She had tremendous fortitude and would sally forth into all parts of the United States equipped with corsets and stays. He had huge respect, as well as affection, for her memory.

He also assured me that no western movie he had ever made had ever involved cruelty to horses. I had read that tripwires were used to cause horses to fall down (in a shooting sequence), but he was most insistant that there were precautions against any animal cruelty. He didn't quite explain how it was done, but I was impressed by his concern, anyway. Gregory Peck was a charming person, and interesting to talk to.

. . . and Marshall McLuhan . . .

Marshall McLuhan was a Canadian professor of English who suddenly – it seemed – became the major media guru of the 1960s. He coined the phrase 'the medium is the message', and wrote scholarly books such as *The Gutenberg Galaxy* and *Understanding Media*. These tomes explained that television wasn't just a new means of communication: it was a different means of communication which would change not just our information basis, but the way in which we related to information, and how this affected our whole perceptions, and politics.

I was in New York in 1967, and cabled the editor of the *Evening Standard* about McLuhan: his name was on everyone's lips, and he was the hot talking point. Instructions came back – 'go and interview him'. So I took a plane to Toronto and saw Professor McLuhan. He was a tall, craggy-faced Canadian with an Ulster-Scots face, gentlemanly manner and a dry, sophisticated wit, slightly bemused by his sudden fame. We had lunch and he wrote a somewhat austere dedication.

I filed the interview and the paper ran it as though it was something very important.

It wasn't anything very important, but it is a revealing episode about how the media works. McLuhan was 'hot': he was the latest novelty and the newest fad, and that is what the media loves – fair play to it. Though I suppose it could be said that Marshall McLuhan was the father of media studies, which have become a major business subsequently.

I had Tea with Grace of Monaco

Princess Grace wrote, or compiled a book about flowers, in which she replicated the flowers that she had pressed into her commonplace book at the toytown palace at Monaco. And on the occasion of the publication of this book, which was brought out by Sidgewick & Jackson, it was arranged that I should do an interview with her for the *Sunday Independent* in Dublin. I think that the late Lord Longford, who was a director of Sidgewick & Jackson, and who was always kind to me and friendly towards anything Irish, may have had a hand in arranging the encounter.

And so I turned up at the Connaught Hotel, and, after enquiring at the desk, was instructed to proceed to her suite, some floors up. I did so, knocked on the door, and she opened it herself, wearing a plaid skirt and a simple, white shirt. She was a little stouter, a little more matronly, than she had been in her exquisite prime, but she looked very pleasant and very well. Tea was presented on a trolley and she carried out the tea-pouring duties herself.

We didn't talk very much about flowers: she spoke about Ireland, about County Mayo, about her family and the values she had picked up from them. She spoke about Philadelphia and said, rather wittily, that one of the reasons why she got along well with the British royal family (and particularly Queen Elizabeth) was that 'they're a lot less snooty than the folks in Philadelphia.' She also recalled how Philadelphia society had been, in her father's time, somewhat excluding to Irish Catholics.

Her Irish roots meant a great deal to Grace of Monaco and she was looking forward to building a family home in County Mayo. Her grandfather, John Henry Kelly was one of those many poor Irish emigrants, driven across the Atlantic at the age of nineteen in search of a new life that would sustain him.

And he found it, working first as a labourer in Vermont and subsequently in New York State. He married a young Irishwoman, aged just seventeen, in 1869, Mary Costello. The couple eventually moved to Philadelphia where, by 1890, they had produced a family of ten children. Grace spoke about the influence that this paternal grandmother had on the subsequent family.

Mothers of large families often grow into strong matriarchs, and Mary Costello Kelly was one such. She ruled her extended family with a mixture of love, faith and ambition. Her youngest son, John Brendan – known as Jack – was to become Grace's father. The last of the family was a daughter, also Grace, from the Irish, *Gráinne* – who died at the age of twenty-two, at the beginning of a promising career in the theatre. An older son, George, became a successful playwright: the Irish leaning towards drama was in the genes.

The first-generation emigrant family never grew rich, but their children rose to success through the discipline, duty and hard work inspired most particularly by Mary Costello Kelly – known as 'the dowager' in the family. She never let them forget their roots and their religion. Nor, later, did they forget the struggle for acceptance in Philadelphia.

The Philadelphia social attitude rankled, though, as did an event in England when Grace's father, Jack, qualified for the Diamond Sculls at Henley in 1919. Jack Kelly – driven by his own and his mother's ambition – had made himself into one of the most accomplished athletes in the world, in the rowing speciality known as sculling. He was obsessive in application and had won many national titles in the US. But he was rejected for the prestigious Henley event – 'because,' Grace told me, 'he had worked with his hands. And a working man could not qualify.' In fact, no official reason was given, but it was evident that the class issue came into play: and very possibly the Irish connection too.

Jack Kelly was to become a rich man – a fortune he built up in the building trade, like many an Irishman before him. He married an attractive and athletic girl – and a champion swimmer – Margaret Majer. Grace was also proud to mention that her mother had been the first woman to teach physical education at the University of Pennsylvania. Jack and Margaret had four children, Grace being the third. She was a sickly child, sometimes overlooked in the middle of a highly sporty and athletic family, and she always felt, all through her life, that she could never quite please her father.

Those who come up the hard way are often hard on themselves and on others: as Yeats wrote – 'too long a sacrifice/Can make a stone of the heart.' And that sense of inborn struggle which was part of the family tradition made Jack Kelly an exacting parent, especially to Grace.

Yet she blossomed into an immensely pretty youngster and from her teenage years, determined to succeed in her chosen career of acting. By her early twenties she was a world-famous film star and an Academy award winner.

It is said of Grace Kelly, as she then was, that her Catholic formation was in conflict with her essentially sensuous nature. This may be so, but an inner conflict can be productive for a creative artist, and if she felt the conflict, it served to refine her performances.

And so, it came about, after filming on location in the South of France, Grace was introduced to Prince Rainier III, and by April 1956, they were married at Monaco Cathedral in a ceremony which was to be the first globalised royal media event. Journalists talked about the Rainier wedding for decades – there was so much world interest that it turned into near-pandemonium. Grace and Rainier were alarmed by the scale of the media interest and often looked back on it with a kind of horror.

And yet, it put Monaco on the map. Few people had heard of the principality before that wedding; afterwards, everyone knew about it. Monaco was, through the marriage with Grace, developed as a world 'brand', and its identity and economy have thrived and developed because of it. France, which from time to time had threatened to absorb the principality, has come to accept Monaco's special status, and even to regard the Grimaldi family as their very own proxy royals, strangely acceptable within the paradox of their Republican tradition.

And if Grace helped to put Monaco on the map, she was also instrumental in opening up Ireland to modernisation. She had always retained an affection for the Irish traditions of her family, and it was with evident joy that she and Prince Rainier arrived in Ireland on June 10, 1961. For fifty years, royalty had been all but anathemised in a society dedicated to austerely republican values. But Grace arrived, not just as a Princess – indeed, it was impressively noted that she was the most titled woman in Europe, being 'twice a princess, four times a duchess, twice a marquise, eight times a countess and five times a baroness' – but as something more welcome in Irish hearts: one of our own.

She was much moved by that experience; and later purchased land in the area where she planned to build a home, though we know now, it was never to be.

The last years of Princess Grace's life were marked by worries over her children – she was very concerned, when I spoke to her, about how we raise our children, and whether we educate them in the right way. She felt particularly strongly that children should not be sent to school before they are seven: she had encountered the Scandinavian system where this is usually the case, and she felt it was much the best. On the raising of children and their care, she struck me as a surprising conservative.

Yet it was sad that her position did not permit her to return to doing more work in the theatre or in cinema. There was something of the lonely housewife about Grace of Monaco, filling up her floral albums with dried flowers and writing letters to old friends. Rainier did not want her to go back to being a movie actress, but she could have done more readings, particularly of poetry, and perhaps more radio and other forms of drama. Had she lived longer – she was only fifty-two when she died – this vocational yearning may have had time to be fulfilled; the Queen of Denmark, after all, is an archeologist and she also produces theatrical set designs. Modern royals are evolving. And I am sure that Grace would also have made a regular home in Ireland, once she felt that her children were more settled.

She certainly was graceful over tea at the Connaught, and I was so absorbed by the event that I quite forgot to ask her to sign her *Book of Flowers*, which I had in my hands.

I had Drinks with Margaret Thatcher

In the 1980s, Prime Minister Margaret Thatcher invited me to 10 Downing Street on several occasions.

She was a welcoming, if slightly brisk, hostess, and would meet me at the reception room with warm words. 'My dear Miss Kenny – I read every word you write.' True or not, it was politically adroit. Later she said, by way of endorsement – 'You Roman Catholics are *so* sound on family values.' If you say so, Prime Minister!

My husband, Richard West, was with me, and he got along hilariously with Maggie's husband, Denis, who was quaffing gin and tonic (or as he'd have called it, G & Ts) at a steady rate. Dennis referred to his wife as 'The Woman', and bent Dick's ear somewhat on what 'The Woman' would or would not let him do.

La Thatcher was always genial on these occasions. At one such drinks party the novelist – great womaniser but also great misogynist – Kingsley Amis was present. He was flirting with Maggie outrageously, and she, indeed, was flirting with him. He referred afterwards to the 'batsqueak of desire' she could inspire in a man. Perhaps especially in the kind of Englishman who likes commanding women, recalling their strict upbringing with Nanny.

Maggie liked men, and especially men in any military form. She was seldom happier than when sitting in a tank surrounded by military chaps.

You couldn't but admire her, because she was a woman of conviction, and she wasn't ashamed of voicing these convictions. This sense of commitment and self-belief she drew from her Methodist father in Grantham, Alderman Roberts.

Work was the ethic most admired: duty was upheld – young Margaret

Roberts, working daily in her father's corner-shop, attended church thrice on Sundays. Her father, Alderman Roberts, would not allow the children's playgrounds of Grantham to be opened on the Sabbath for lest play should promulgate frivolity.

Mrs Thatcher championed capitalism – she carried a copy of Frederick Hayek in her handbag – but she also believed in the Protestant virtues of reward for hard work. Aged nine, she won a school prize for recitation: when a teacher congratulated her on her good fortune, the little moppet replied: 'I wasn't lucky – I deserved it.'

She had a blind spot about Ireland, which I think to some degree also derived from her upbringing. She didn't trust the Irish and she didn't understand the complexities of Irish history. Her press officer during the 1980s was Bernard Ingham, a blunt Yorkshireman who I had known as a journalist on the *Guardian*, and I don't think Bernard really helped Maggie's narrow viewpoint on Ireland, as he shared something of the same mindset.

Although she professed to admire my columns, she refused, resolutely, my requests to do an interview about Anglo-Irish relations. I said to Bernard, several times in the early 1980s, that it was a subject which must be taken seriously, and should be central to the prime minister's agenda. But after Bobby Sands, and particularly after the Brighton Bomb, she was more stubbornly resistant than ever.

Her oft-quoted view that 'Ulster was as British as Finchley' was ludicrous. If Ulster was as Jewish as Finchley, it would be rather more intellectual and a lot better at patronising the arts.

Maggie might have thought that 'You Roman Catholics are sound on family values', but her father didn't favour what he regarded as Roman Catholic nations – he was a stern sabbatarian who closed the playgrounds of Grantham on a Sunday – and most particularly set her against the French, as he believed they were a sinister combination of Roman Catholic, Communist and sexually incontinent.

There was an occasion when Garret Fitzgerald and Francois Mitterand were seated near to Maggie at a European dinner: Fitzgerald and Mitterand spoke French to one other, discussing the novels of Georges Bernanos and Francois Mauriac, which greatly irked Maggie.

The chemistry between herself and Garret wasn't right, and she humiliated him politically with her famous 'Out! Out! Out!' But Charlie Haughey, who seldom failed to exercise a degree of charm on women, got her to the negotiating table, though their political values were chalk and cheese.

Despite her 'Iron Lady' character, Maggie liked to be treated as a woman. That was one of the reasons why she got along so well in Poland, and with the Poles. Admittedly, most of the Poles she met were anti-Communist (and she also felt that Poland had been sold down the river after the Second World War, at the Yalta Conference, when it was more or less handed over to Stalin), but there was another element in the mix, too: the Polish hand-kiss.

Polish gallantry has never abandoned the practice of kissing the hand of a married woman on introduction, and when Maggie travelled to Poland – looking fetching in a fox-fur hat – she was lavishly hand-kissed. It didn't go amiss.

Margaret Thatcher was a political and monetary conservative, but in some areas she was a liberal: she voted for homosexual law reform, and for abortion rights (but against easy divorce, although she had married a divorced man herself – Denis had had a brief wartime marriage that was dissolved – a fact that was kept very discreet until unveiled by the gossip writer Nigel Dempster).

As we know, she was greatly loathed as well as greatly admired. Feminists often deplored her, contending that no real woman could be 'right-wing'. Yet every woman who advances in politics today – and arguably in corporate life too – owes something to Margaret Thatcher. She showed that a woman could do it: not only rise to the top, but become one of the three most influential British prime ministers of the twentieth century. Only Churchill and Lloyd George rank alongside her in the pantheon.

She showed that female leadership could come in all shapes and sizes: it did not have to be an ideology of the collectivist left. Yet perhaps her life also demonstrated that it is not easy to be a warm mother (perhaps a good parent) and an obsessive politician. One of the most telling details of her personal life was that neatness, tidiness and order were major priorities. She would not allow her children to have a pet dog, because dogs are messy. She destroyed virtually all her own archives and letters purely out of 'tidiness'.

When she died, there was the natural sense of mourning at the passing of a great figure. But there were also those who ascribed some blame to 'Thatcherism' for the divisions of society, the destruction of old jobs, and the onset of the slump, along with the odious level of bankers' greed.

Yet, although she believed in free enterprise and the market system, Maggie was never of the 'loadsamoney' bonus culture. The strict Methodism in which she grew up spurned greed as avidly as it damned sloth or squalor.

Perhaps it will take some historical perspective to come to a final judgement on all these debates. Still, I remember those soirées at 10 Downing Street genially: no other prime minister, or indeed Taoiseach, has ever done so, and I am duly grateful to Margaret Thatcher for her hospitality.

Michael Fassbender Acted in My Play

When the celebrated actor and comedian Mel Smith died in July 2013, I remembered how thrilled I had been when Mel made it known that he really liked a play I had written about Winston Churchill and Michael Collins – and was keen to act in it. He had been shown the script by Brian Gilbert, the film, theatre and TV director, who had become my friend too after he had directed a TV documentary about William Joyce, Lord Haw-Haw, from my biography, *Germany Calling*.

I am a stage-struck adolescent at heart and nothing is more gratifying to a writer than hearing that an actor likes something one has written.

Back in 2003, my husband, Richard, had read a biography of Winston Churchill called *The Last Lion*, by William Manchester. Manchester was a journalist, not an academic, and while using the Churchill archives properly, he also had an eye for the human story. And there was one human story that Richard thought would interest me especially: a passage about Churchill and Collins getting drunk together one night in 1921 during the negotiations that were to lead to the Anglo-Irish Treaty in 1922, and eventually, the foundation of the Irish state.

Though initially opponents, Collins and Churchill had that kind of bonding session which men sometimes experience, and subsequently Churchill was firm in his resolve to support the Irish Free State, though he was much disparaged in the House of Commons for doing so.

It struck me immediately that this was a play. I began to research the biographies and contemporary archives and indeed, the period, the characters and events were all utterly fascinating. Since a most contentious aspect of the Anglo-Irish Treaty that followed was the oath of allegiance to the King, which the Irish disliked and the British insisted on, I called the play *Allegiance*: but there was also that double sense of an allegiance between men who have spent a night drinking together.

Brian Gilbert had been interested in the play from the start, and we had a rehearsed reading at the library of Reform Club in London, in which Mel played Churchill and Brendan Coyle played Collins. (Brendan Coyle was a respected actor who became renowned, subsequently, as Mr Bates in *Downton Abbey*.) Arnold Rosen, an energetic clubman at the Reform, acted as impresario who made the performance possible.

And then the occasion arose, through the suggestion of my friend and journalist Carol Sarler, that we might take *Allegiance* to Edinburgh in 2006. It was a hugely exciting prospect, and I set out to raise £8,000 to support the endeavour (and Mel Smith, too, generously helped by not taking any fee and entertaining the company with largesse). Many donors were very generous, including the late Josephine Hart, Herbert Kretzmer, my dear friend Michael Harlick, the author Freddy Forsyth, Gemma Hussey in Dublin and other Irish friends who preferred to remain anonymous (including the late Maeve Binchy, who was generous, but I gathered rather pestered with begging letters. She hated having to turn people down, but felt she couldn't donate to everything).

But who was to play Michael Collins? Brian, as director, set about casting. He was keen for Brendan Coyle to reprise the role but Mr Coyle was otherwise engaged. Through the late spring and summer of 2006 – the play was to go on in August at the Assembly, one of Edinburgh's most prestigious locations– Brian searched for an actor to play Mick. Brian had discovered Jude Law, casting him as Bosie to Stephen Fry's Oscar Wilde in the movie he directed about Oscar and spotted the talents, too, of Michael Sheen early on.

And it was through the advice of an experienced casting agent who was familiar with the Irish scene, Ros Hubbard, that the name of Michael Fassbender came up. He had been in *Band of Brothers* and was known as a promising young actor. Was he free? Would he do it? Actors don't make much money in Edinburgh, but it is a wonderful showcase. Yes, he would, but the agreement was made so late that Michael's name wasn't even on the posters advertising *Allegiance*. It was Mel, as Churchill, who was the focal point.

* * *

As it happened, the opening of *Allegiance* was a sensation, because Mel Smith was prepared to smoke a Churchillian cigar on stage, in defiance of the newly-introduced anti-smoking ban, which was implemented with particularly ferocious Calvinist fervour by Edinburgh Council.

The cigar was an authentic part of the interchange between Collins and Churchill, and made a specific point. But the Edinburgh authorities threatened to close down the entire festival if Mel lit that cigar. The episode made headlines all around the world, which brought huge publicity to the event, although, despite Sam Goldwyn's adage, there is such a thing as the wrong kind of publicity. If everyone is focused on the sensation involved, nobody is focused on the substance.

Mel came very near to lighting the cigar, but didn't quite. And *Allegiance* proceeded. And altogether it got some very good reviews, full houses – 400 people attending each performance – and at one point a standing ovation. It was all hugely exciting, and to echo Winston Churchill, I felt, personally, that 'the whole of my life was a preparation for this hour, and I am walking with destiny.'

What was most thrilling about the experience was the chemistry that existed between Mel Smith and Michael Fassbender on stage. (Brian Gilbert acted as reader linking the scenes, and Robin Browne very ably played Winston's butler.) Mel really got the big-baby side of Winston as a man of forty-six – a man who had never dressed himself, who blubbed very easily, and who had just been through two personal bereavements which had affected him deeply. And Michael was unsurpassable as Collins.

Though he lacked the physical beefiness of Collins, Fassender was able to act the physical impact: he was able to combine the outer warrior with the inner man who often suffered anguish over violence. He understood Collins' charisma and sex-appeal, and also his brooding side, his contradictions – a leader who, for two pins, would have shot the Bishop of Cork for opposing Sinn Féin, but who, daily, lit candles and even attended Mass at the Catholic church in Maiden Lane and at Brompton Oratory.

A man of humour, and of rough play, who called forth adulation from Hazel Lavery and inspired her husband, Sir John, to paint Collins as

Hercules; a man who knew he was on a mission for which he would probably pay with his life, and yet who felt he must do his duty. Michael Fassbender internalised all that and then brought it all out in his acting. And between him and Mel there was a spark of humour which was terrific.

I wrote in my diary at the time: 'A stage magic appeared, that chemistry which brings a drama to life, in which the characters take on a life of their own. I began by being thrilled to hear the text I had written by actors, but then, it was as if I was watching something that someone else was bringing something to me. Such assured performances by Mel, Michael and Brian . . .

Michael's parents – his German father and Irish mother – came over from Killarney to see the performance and they were lovely people. Michael struck me as a hugely dedicated actor, and yet an uncomplicated kind of guy. He had no pretensions and laughed easily. He was warm and friendly and good company. He was, it was said, one for the ladies, and sometimes one for a night – or all night – on the town. I confided to my diary that he was 'an absolute dish': had I been thirty years younger I'd have developed a real crush. He was, however, charming to me, and even after late partying, always sober and professional on stage. Acting mattered to him; doing the job right came first.

He has since risen and risen in the firmament and has become a global star of the first rank. He was superb as the Bobby Sands character in *Hunger*, greatly praised for his role in *Shame*, outstanding as Karl Jung in *The Dangerous Method*, and a compelling Mr Rochester in *Jane Eyre*. To me, he will always be my Michael Collins and I owe a debt of gratitude to Mel Smith for his enthusiasm, and to Brian Gilbert for bringing Mel and Michael together in such an unforgettable way.

The Queen Complimented Me
And Gerry Adams kissed me

In 2011 – a hundred years after the last royal state visit by a British monarch – Queen Elizabeth II came to the Republic of Ireland, and although access and visibility was sadly so denied to the public because of security measures, it turned out to be a happy and successful occasion. Having written a book about Ireland's relationship with the British monarchy – *Crown and Shamrock: Love and Hate between Ireland and the British Monarchy* – I had reported the visit for the *Irish Independent*, the *Spectator*, the *Daily Telegraph*, RTÉ and sundry media outlets.

On Wednesday 18 May, the British Ambassador, Julian King laid on a glamorous gathering by the Liffey for the Queen and Prince Philip, at the National Convention Centre in Dublin, which is like a half-tilted biscuit tin made of glass. It was a balmy early-summer evening, and the centre was very full and very good-tempered, and arrangements were made so that various guests could meet Elizabeth and Philip. I was lined up with a group of writers, between Colm Tóibín and Sebastian Barry, and when HM came to our little group, Colm, being the leader of our section, presented me. 'This is Mary Kenny, a journalist and writer . . .' I duly shook hands with HM and said, 'I hope you saw some nice Irish horses today, Ma'am,' since she had that afternoon visited the National Stud.

She replied that she had, indeed. Then she suddenly smiled rather shyly at me and said, altogether spontaneously, 'I enjoyed your article in yesterday's newspaper very much.' It was the shyness of her smile which really beguiled; I felt that she hadn't been 'briefed' to say this, but that it was a spontaneous remark. I had indeed written a long piece in the *Daily*

Telegraph the previous day, whose theme, drawn on *Crown and Shamrock*, was why this royal visit could not have taken place until 2011. The Queen is known to be a *Telegraph* reader (she also likes the crossword).

What journalist isn't pleased to be told that an article is appreciated? And of course I was gratified. The Queen seemed so kind and thoughtful. The evening proceeded and it was a terrific success, especially when Elizabeth went up on stage to talk to the entertainers, and most especially Mary Byrne, a favourite songstress who had won fame through the *X Factor*, having previously been a check-out lady in Tesco of Ballyfermot.

* * *

More than six months later, in December 2011, I attended a book launch party at the National Museum in Dublin. The book was Jimmy Deenihan's autobiography *My Sporting Life*, being an enjoyable and valuable account of Jimmy's life as a GAA champion – a real record of his sporting activities. Jimmy Deenihan is the Minister for the Arts in the coalition Fine Gael-Labour government, an honest and decent politician, modest in his way of life (he never indulged in fancy expenses claims), dedicated to his native Kerry, and imaginative in his approach to the arts. For his party, the museum's ceramics room was heaving with people; Jimmy is popular and the clans had gathered for his support.

I purchased my book and went to the line to ask him to sign it when suddenly Gerry Adams, the Sinn Féin leader, hoved into view, and seeing me, swooped and bestowed a kiss upon my cheek. I was (perhaps literally) gobsmacked: but I'm a polite convent girl at heart and I reacted cordially.

When I don't quite know what to say to someone, I say, 'how's the family', so I said 'how's the family?' and Gerry started talking amicably about his three little granddaughters. I said then that I thought Martin McGuinness had done well in his bid to stand for president (there had just been a presidential election) and Gerry said, yes, he'd done very well and they were all very pleased. And then we came to the top of the line and friendly words were again exchanged as we parted, and I approached Jimmy to autograph my copy of his book.

I pondered, though, why Gerry Adams had kissed me. I came to the conclusion, first, that this showed he had now grown into a confident member of the Dáil. (He had also said 'I always read your pieces' – a slight variation on the Queen's compliment, but nonetheless flattering.). Irish politicians are affable and glad-handing: that's their style. He had graduated from a flinty Northerner to a blarneying southerner, possibly. He was, anyway, elected. My late friend Mary Holland always predicted that he would take this course and would eventually come to dominate Dublin politics. He has not dominated, but Adams has become integrated and is a recognisable figure (though he certainly still has his critics, especially in association with previous IRA activities).

I have written critically – indeed, with some hostility – about Sinn Féin in the past, but I have also welcomed their entry into constitutional politics. I sincerely welcomed Martin McGuinness's decision to run for president and wrote that in the *Irish Independent* (and I was impressed by McGuinness's ecumenism, working with Protestant clerics, and attending the funeral of Iris Robinson's mother in a Free Presbyterian church where, previously, no Roman Catholic had ever trod. He was greeted with applause).

I am, in a slightly quirky way, an all-Ireland anti-partitionist. Edward Carson, too, had been an anti-partitionist and refused to attend the opening of Stormont in 1932 for that reason. But I believe that an all-Ireland entity should be a diverse Ireland, with tolerance and respect for all our traditions, nationalist and unionist, Catholic and Protestant, republican and monarchist, and that the best way of pursuing this is through democratic constitutionalism.

Perhaps in receiving a kindly compliment from the Queen, and a kiss from Gerry Adams within the same year, I had achieved a personal notch of inclusiveness.

Part Three
Absent Friends

Terry Keane
Ireland's Madame De Pompadour

When Terry Keane died in 2008, my niece Marie-Louise was crestfallen. Marie-Louise had worked with Terry as her researcher and sometimes co-writer, and had come to love her. Terry, she said, was as a great and exotic wild bird who brought a unique sense of colour into life.

Terry was someone who elicited extreme opinions. Those who knew and loved her saw Terry as a beacon of laughter, generosity and allure. Her critics saw a different Terry. A close advisor to Charlie Haughey told me 'don't mention that woman's name to me: she is poison.' It was, of course, known that Terry was C. J. Haughey's mistress for many years, before and during his term as Taoiseach. It was a known fact among his circle, members of the media – my friend June Levine lent the pair her apartment for trysts – and other *cognoscenti*. It was suspected among a wider public, but there are things that people don't mind suspecting, but they don't entirely want to know.

Terry was adored, but she was also criticised, even by some of her closest friends. 'Terry is the most selfish woman in the world,' one of her oldest friends told me. 'A typical only child!' With apologies to only children – there is a belief that some never quite learn that the world doesn't revolve around them. Terry (born Teresa O'Donnell) was the only child of successful Irish doctors who had migrated to England, where she partly grew up. The advantage of being an only child, it is said, is that all the confidence and parental expectations are transmitted to the child. Terry certainly had a sense of entitlement that demanded the best of everything. She could have been the origin of the L'Oreal advert, 'Because I'm worth it!' But she was worth it.

We are all a mixture of attributes. Yet I think both critics and friends of Terry would agree about one thing: she was a genuine, a real, a true femme fatale.

The authentic femme fatale is not necessarily a woman of outstanding beauty, or even very evident sex appeal. 'Pulling' guys is not what the true femme fatale does: almost any female under fifty (and many well over it) can 'pull' if she puts her mind to it.

The true femme fatale is something else: men are profoundly smitten by her spell. They will risk their life, their career, their family for her enchantment – as Charles J. Haughey did. And that was a phenomenal talent of Terry's. Men were smitten by her to a point of obsession.

I once walked into the apartment of a very senior Irish civil servant in Brussels, (now also no longer with us). This man was making policy for Ireland in the realm of foreign affairs. He was terrifically brainy and good company too. There was only one picture on his walls: a tastefully naked photograph of Terry Keane, taken from the curvature of her beautiful back. Before this picture, this mandarin worshipped. That is what a femme fatale is: she exercises a power of witchcraft. She was also wildly daring.

On another occasion, I was with Terry at an event at the (alas, now defunct) Royal Hibernian Hotel on Dawson Street – this must have been around 1970 – and we were drinking with a group of guys in a kind of lounge-bar afterwards, and someone dared Terry to strip naked (to the waist), which she immediately did with great elan. I felt I'd be a wuss if I didn't do likewise, but reader, I assure you, it didn't have the same effect.

She was, in her prime, stylish and audacious. That confidence! But unlike the aforementioned Irish diplomat (who had no books in his apartment save for the dreary *Economist*) she was cultivated – almost an imperative for the great court mistresses, just like Madame de Pompadour. She knew about art and antiques and old silver and porcelain. She had a refined and educated taste in the decorative arts. She knew about wines and their provenance, and in an era when most of us were knocking back any old plonk, Terry knew about Chateau Margaux and Montrachet (one of hers – and Charlie's – favourites.)

Charlie Haughey is a major character in Gerard Stembridge's engaging novel of the 1970s *The Effect of Her*, (and I am a minor character, thankfully – thankful to be minor, that is). In this narrative, Terry's style is represented as something that Charlie very much aspires to: he's the gurrier who wants to be gentry.

He likes the fact that a toady has organised a Knightsbridge apartment for his sojourns in London, rather than a posh hotel. Charlie thinks:

> A woman like Terry would appreciate the greater discretion and privacy. It would also be no harm to let her see what favours he could still command, what influence he still possessed . . . Such was the extravagant ambition of the interior design, the space, the luxury, atmosphere and grandeur of the views, he and Terry might not want to leave the apartment at all. And, from what he recalled, the bed looked like it would take a lot of punishment. Harrods could deliver.

But Charlie (in the novel) is in error if he thinks Terry is a woman of discretion: the fictional protagonist in the story, Mags, knows Terry and reflects that 'Terry could no more have resisted talking about this affair among her friends than she could have stopped breathing. What would have been the point of a secret if it couldn't be shared with someone? That very merry night at June's place, Terry's references to the great secret, initially coy, had become gradually more suggestion, and at last, hilariously outrageous.'

Yet Terry had something else for which men will sometimes shoot themselves: she was funny. She was a brilliant raconteur, her stories told and embellished in that seductively contralto voice. She could tell you a story to your face in which you were the butt of the anecdote, and still you would laugh: you would not only be amused but flattered. She told an entertaining story about me, which was both teasing and flattering. It was entertaining mainly because of the way in which Terry recounted it, though spoken wit doesn't always translate to print.

Terry and I were out on the razzle one night and like much of my misspent youth, I have no recollection whatsoever of where we went or what we did. An alcoholic's memory is – perhaps an unusual kindness of Nature, or the Almighty, like the shorn lamb being sheltered from the wind – hazed over with a welcome retrospective mist. According to Terry, anyway, we were staggering at 3 AM, and I suggested that she stay in my flat in Ballsbridge, rather than make her way to Killiney, where she lived. And so we fell into the deep sleep of those who have had far, far too much champagne and Montrachet, which I'm sure Terry insisted upon.

We were both in party clothes and when we awoke the next morning, Terry said she'd look into my wardrobe to see if there was anything suitable to wear for a working day. Apparently, she couldn't find anything there which wasn't completely inappropriate for sober wear, and so she had to don her party clothes again for a business meeting. It was the way in which she described the vignette, and the way in which the outrageous silliness of my wardrobe emerged that made it so droll.

But there can be a sad side to a great conversationalist: you may outshine to the psychological detriment of others. After a particularly hilarious lunch with Terry and some friends in Chelsea in the late 1990s, I remarked to her son, Tim, as we drove away: 'Your mother is full of personality.'

'Yes,' Tim said in a small voice. 'I sometimes think that she has so much personality there was none left over for me.' Tim was a gifted but fragile individual, and he died alone after a domestic accident in 2004. Terry suffered dreadfully over that.

And actually, she was an intensely family-minded person. She adored her children and grandchildren and was devastated when a newborn baby granddaughter died. Terry voted the pro-life ticket in the 1983 referendum on abortion; she had, after all, valiantly placed her first child for adoption rather than avail of an abortion (and how happy she was, later, to be reconciled with that much-loved daughter). Terry also voted against introducing divorce in the referenda. To the day she died she was still married to her husband, Judge Ronan Keane.

I know it sounds strange, but a mistress may be supportive of the family structure. Her politics were also a bit strange: she was a strong Irish nationalist and Republican – but she was also completely *au fait* with grandee English and aristocratic life, and totally at ease in that milieu. She (and her husband) sent their son, Tim to a posh English Catholic boarding school (where he wasn't happy), and he too had that melange of politics of vehement Irish nationalism with a patina of English upper-class mores. Many is the argument I had with Tim – who was very friendly with Marie-Louise – over that political subject which dominated our discourses in the 1970s and 1980s: Northern Ireland and the validity of a campaign of violence to rid the province of 'the Brits'.

* * *

Yet Terry was surely ill-advised to allow herself to be pressurised into selling her story about her relationship with Charlie Haughey. There is an old French tradition which holds that whatever matrimonial sins you commit, you do not publicly embarrass the spouse or the children – that was part of supporting the family structure. Terry came to regret that decision, and yet, bewilderingly, she repeated the exercise, even after the apology.

The femme fatale is high-maintenance, and her fine taste in lifestyle requires revenue. And that, I think, clouded the judgement. We all have a prevailing weakness, and Terry's, I think, was money, though I don't think she made a lot of money from her autobiographical endeavours, sold initially to the Irish edition of the *Sunday Times*. She also appeared on *The Late Late Show* revealing her relationship with Charlie. That did shock people – not out of prudishness, I think, but because it must have been hurtful for Maureen Haughey, and Charlie Haughey's four children (who maintained a continuing position of dignity and decorum through all these perturbations).

The situation being so public must, indeed, have been hurtful for Mrs Haughey, and it is reported that she is writing her own version of all these events, with the encouragement of her family. Maureen Haughey is the daughter of a very fine Irish politician, and sometime Taoiseach, Sean Lemass, who succeeded Eamon de Valera – and should have succeeded him a lot sooner – and sought to modernise Ireland's economy in the 1950s. I have interviewed Mrs Haughey and she seemed a very pleasant person and was an exemplary wife to Charlie.

And yet, I don't believe that Charlie's relationship with Terry was – as some have supposed – a superficial one based on sex and Chateau Margaux. I believe that Charlie was mad about Terry, and seemed to need her. I spent a long weekend with Terry and Noelle Campbell-Sharp at

Noelle's artist's colony in Killreelig in County Kerry in the late 1990s: it was just before the era of the ubiquitous mobile phone, and the house phone rang all day, it seemed to me, as Charlie called Terry from his holiday island of Inishvickilaun.

Terry took the calls but sometimes there was a barely perceptible roll of the eyes. We walked on the beach with her little dog, and I got the impression that she was beginning to find her lover very needy.

It would take a book to describe the charms and complexities of Terry Keane, and someday someone will write it. I hope it may be done with the beguilement which so personified the lady herself. My niece Marie-Louise Kenny travelled widely with Terry and she, I think, may come to do that biography one day.

Nuala Fennell

From housewife to politician

I was at the Hotel Meurice in Calais when I heard about Nuala Fennell's death in 2009. I had seen her relatively recently and she had seemed well, so it was a shock as well as a loss. Nuala had a blood condition which necessitated transfusions every few months, but she made light of it. Yet it wore down her heart and she died, surrounded by her family, aged seventy-three. Nuala Fennell was a significant feminist and politician in Irish modern history. She launched an organisation, AIM, to give women and children enforceable rights to the family home and income. She campaigned for victims of domestic violence with Irish Women's Aid, and with the Women's Political Association. She was the first minister of state for Women's Affairs in an Irish administration, and she was instrumental in abolishing the legal construct of 'illegitimacy' in the Irish state.

What was impressive about Nuala's political career was that she started out, in 1977, without contacts or connections: without dynastic links to any major political party. Her first political endeavours involved going around knocking on doors and canvassing political support when she was a housewife.

The conversation that I had with my mother about this situation, in the 1970s, was revealing about contrasting attitudes in Irish life. 'Hasn't she a great nerve,' Ma said, 'entering politics like that when no one belonging to her is in political life?'

'But that makes her all the more wonderful, Ma,' I remonstrated. 'So much more democratic!'

My mother was not impressed; she possibly thought that Nuala's inde-pendent bid for a political career was too forward; or not feminine; or that a person – and particularly a woman – should have some kinship link with political life before entering it. Politics in Ireland has a tradition of being dynastic, and following family traditions was admired (maybe particularly in the West of Ireland, where my mother's roots were, and where clan mat-ters a great deal.)

We are all influenced in our choices by our mothers – influenced to be different from them, or to follow them. Nuala made plain in her memoir, *Political Woman* (finished just three weeks before she died) that she was contra-influenced by her mother's life. She definitely didn't want to be like her mother, who had had a lively and stimulating life as a single woman – working, going to the theatre, playing tennis – only to be buried, subse-quently, in a lonely and restricted life as the wife of a police officer who moved around the country.

> Cut-off, without next-door neighbours like other wives, she was bored and restless and read numerous books from the local library . . . I remember being sad for my mother: she did all the cooking, cleaning and shopping. She was weighed down. Young as I was, at around the age of ten, I questioned why she could not have changed her life, be a person as well as a mother. I resolved that motherhood alone would not be my destiny . . .

This is a common theme of feminists of my generation, and of other generations too: that they wanted more from life than the restrictions they had seen imposed on their mothers – though I disagree with Nuala's sup-position that this was a particularly Irish condition. American feminist lit-erature is full of these reflections and reactions. I had some of the same feelings about my mother's life, although for me, it was more about money, as I recall. Even in old-fashioned 1950s Ireland, women with financial means (or substantial dowries) were always more emancipated, and acted with a certain sense of entitlement, too.

Nuala was a wonderful woman and I was terribly upset to hear of her – to me – sudden death. She writes warmly about me in her memoir and claims that it was I who first urged her to commit to feminism; and in that I am honoured. She also says – alas, that we can no longer have any sparky arguments about this – that she could never 'fathom' how I could have revised my views about a range of values, including some aspects of feminism.

And I think this is because Nuala was essentially a virtuous woman, and an irreproachable wife. I am certain she would never have had an affair – actually, I know that her married life was exceptionally happy and fulfilled, sexually and in every other dimension. When she was a minister of this state, she gave an interview to *Hot Press* on the joys of orgasm and although she later wondered if that was imprudent, I thought it spoke well for the experiences of her own life.

But being essentially a virtuous woman and an irreproachable wife, perhaps Nuala found it harder to 'fathom' those of us who are, at heart, more inclined to be floosies. We know, through the emotional car-crashes of our own lives that unless society – be it through law, custom, community or taboo – imposes some boundaries and controls, values will be weakened and moral restraints broken. I didn't, in the end, find the experiments of 'permissive society' congenial, and I saw and experienced how much confusion followed. Moreover, when you are the mother of sons, you begin to see the problems that men encounter: they are not all 'patriarchs', and looking back at my childhood now with a little more honesty, perhaps, than I had in my prime, I can see how difficult life could be for men, too. *Pace* Tammy Wynette, sometimes it's hard to be a man.

Nuala's lifelong marriage to Brian was, to me, the epitome of social as well as conjugal virtue: what is more useful to society than a couple who stay faithful, raise children in a successful and stable home, live to see the fruits of their love and commitment unto the third generation, producing well-balanced and useful members of society? And this stability and virtue was built on the steady example given both by Nuala's parents and by Brian's, who embodied, in their lives, the virtuous aspirations of many of our parents, often with some element of sacrifice.

Nuala was almost mystified, in restrospect, that she and Brian didn't live together before marriage – didn't, indeed, have sex before marriage. At the end of her life, they thought their own decorousness both hilarious and antiquated. But speaking for the floosey tendency, isn't there something to be said for building up a steady courtship through love, flirtation, gradual familiarity and certain restraints, so that when the couple come to the marriage bed, their erotic passions are aroused but not spent? Certainly, Jewish tradition would make that claim, since orthodox Jews forbid conjugal intercourse on certain days of the month (for up to seven days after a menstrual period). I have been told that this practice makes for a passionate marriage-bed, and elements of such restraints are used by therapists treating sexual dysfunction.

The paradox in Nuala's story is that the opinions she affirms are often at odds with the evidence she offers. For example, she castigates the limitations of the Irish convent school education – and indeed, she is absolutely correct in saying that in her youth science and maths were often poorly taught to young women. And yet, personally, she was much encouraged by the Dominican nuns at Eccles Street, praised for her English essays, and encouraged to write by a particular nun.

She – again, quite justifiably – castigates the influence of the Catholic church on Irish life at many junctures; she especially loathes Fianna Fáil for the way in which it kow-tows to the church – or did, in the past – although the truth is that all political parties kow-tow to power of any description, and when churches are full to overflowing, as they may still be at a funeral or a special occasion, that is a form of power that successful politicians instinctively recognise. (She admits, for example, that even the more progressive elements of Fine Gael still canvassed for votes after country Masses.)

And again, some of the personal evidence is at odds with her overall generalisations: some individual priests couldn't have been more helpful or supportive – she cites the late Fr Fergal O'Connor, who co-founded Ally, an organisation to support single mothers, in 1971 and Father Chris Crowley, of Whitefrair Street Church, who, with Brian Fennell, helped set up a group to try and get male domestic abusers to come and speak about their patterns of violence. This was in the 1970s, well before domestic violence was quite so highlighted.

Nuala's memoir should really be called 'from desperate housewife to government minister', because that was her life path, and it is certainly an inspiration, from many points of view. The great thing about Nuala was that she *wasn't* a member of the 'political class', but she broke through the system by sheer dedication, hard work and family support.

And here's that contradiction again: Nuala absolutely affirmed herself as a feminist, and so she was. But it's clear that what really changed her life, and in every way for the better, was getting married, and to a good man. Her life before meeting Brian was, as she describes it, dull and boring in a dead-end office job. It was, in that respect, the opposite of her mother's life, which had been active and lively before marriage, but dull and dreary afterwards.

With Nuala, it was meeting Brian at nineteen and marrying him at twenty-two that opened up the rest of her active, energetic, generous and crusading career. She describes Brian as her 'salvation'. Nuala disparages the aspiration that was held out for young women to make a good marriage, and yet, in her own life, she couldn't have shown more dazzlingly the fulfilment of such a destiny.

And that gift lasted right to the end of her life. As she approached death, her husband and loving family – children and grandchildren – were all around her: they were all so close, they embraced so tenderly and told her how much they loved her, and she said how wonderful it had all been and how much she had enjoyed it all and how she loved them. It was a perfect death after a life of good cheer and usefulness. Who could ask for more?

The Shock of Departure
Poem for Nuala

The dead stay with you when they depart
Their aura remains: awhile:
It pulls at your heart
And invades your chromosomes.

John Donne, too, hovers
With that *aide-memoire*
That no man is an isle
Aye: and no woman either.
And yes, a piece of your life has indeed gone
With a friend's departure.
And the dead are there, beckoning
For you: for they've not disappeared
But gone before.

Yet it is a dark reckoning
With life's end – for some:
The bitter rue of past regrets and missed chances –
Bad choices and cheap romances . . .
But not for her: she died with grace
Among her own
Sweetly making her farewells.
'I love you all. Take care of one another.'
Christ-like in its resonance and perfection –
All, all had been accomplished.

For her, the bell tolls joyfully
Telling of a life fulfilled.
But I feel a clod of earth fall away
And I am lessened.

August 2009

Mary Holland
From fashion to politics

When Mary Holland died, in June 2004, her humanist funeral service in Dublin was attended by two Nobel prize winners: Seamus Heaney, the poet, and John Hume, sometime leader of the mainly nationalist SDLP party in Northern Ireland, among many other dignitaries.

Seamus Heaney said, in tribute to Mary, that 'unusually for a journalist', she had had an influence on the events of her lifetime. 'In the Yeatsian sense, she was one of the "hearers and heartners of the work", in both the cultural and the political worlds.'

Mary Holland was widely acknowledged as an influential political journalist, who was instrumental in bringing to worldwide attention the troubling events in Northern Ireland in the late 1960s. I remember covering the British general election in Liverpool in February 1974: we were at the Adelphi Hotel where the political bigwigs were amassing. Harold Wilson entered the lobby, and immediately made his way over to where Mary was standing, to shake her hand. Wilson told her that she had concentrated his mind considerably on the issue of Northern Ireland.

I heard him tell her how much he admired her reportage from Ireland, and what a key influence it had had on him, and the Labour administration. What I recall at the time – Mary might not have thanked me for mentioning this, though she would never deny a fact – was that she was wearing an exquisite mink coat, flawlessly cut. Mary's journalistic roots were, after all, in fashion: she always had immaculate taste and she had been married to a man who could afford to provide his wife with a mink coat. Archaic values now, but at one time, they counted!

Her critics might have claimed that Mary's sympathies for the nationalist underdog – which Harold Wilson clearly admired – was partisan. But she always strove to be fair in her reportage, and at the end of her writing life, in the 1990s, she was at pains to highlight the Loyalist and Unionist side of the Northern Ireland story. As Seamus Heaney said, her efforts to be fair to all sides were exemplary. 'She had a probity that rubbed off on people.'

Mary Philomena Holland was born in England, in Dover in 1935, when her parents were briefly resident in Maidenhead. Her family had originated in Clonakilty, West Cork but her father, Patrick, a lieutenant colonel in the Royal Engineers, was posted to Malaya (where he designed bridges). Mary's two elder brothers had been born in Malaya, whither her parents returned when Mary was an infant.

As a young child – barely out of babyhood - Mary was despatched to Ireland to live with an aunt in County Cork, who was a nun. Still very young, she was sent to Loreto Convent in Rathfarnham, Dublin, and subsequently to a convent at Farnborough in Hampshire. In later years she often spoke of having been at convent boarding school 'since the age of three'.

Although the nuns were not unkind to her – Loreto, Rathfarnham was a very grand place and the 'mother-house' of the Loreto order in Ireland – she came to feel that the early separation from her parents and siblings brought emotional problems. She spoke to me about emotions having been 'cauterised' by the experience. And she was a person of stoical temperament, who never responded to the 'touchy-feely' element in late twentieth-century culture, and could be wittily venomous about writers who went in for 'touchy-feely' prose or sought self-pity: she couldn't stand Nuala O'Faolain, whose autobiography, *Are You Somebody?* was somewhat in this genre (she was acidly critical of Nuala O'Faolain's 'mawkish' writing). Mary was warm of heart but she was not a person for hugs and kisses.

Mary's brothers, John and Bill, both became doctors, and she studied briefly for a law degree at King's College in London, but she dropped out of university to become a journalist after winning a competition for young writers with *Vogue* magazine at the age of eighteen. At *Vogue*, she developed her interest in the theatre and the arts, and interviewed such glittering celebrities as Sir Laurence Olivier and Vanessa Redgrave. She also wrote for *Queen* magazine and *Plays and Players*. Impressed by a profile that she had written of the poet, Philip Larkin, David Astor of the Observer hired her, and he became a guiding mentor in her journalistic development.

Initially, Mary wrote about the arts – she stood in for Kenneth Tynan as theatre critic (who she remembered as being infallibly kind to her) and struck up a good friendship with Penelope Gilliatt, the film critic and sometime wife of John Osborne. She became, for a time, fashion editor of the *Observer*, in which role she combined aspirational high couture with an eye for a bargain.

The first time I met Mary was in Notting Hill Gate in the late 1960s, where she had a boho-chic flat – a kind of cottage tucked away in Palace Gardens Terrace, not far from Notting Hill Gate tube station. I was brought there by an Irish publisher, and was somewhat in awe of the smart set associated with Ken Tynan and the *Observer*. (Not long afterwards, I was interviewed by an editorial panel at the *Observer* with a view to appointing me woman's editor: but they decided that I was 'too left-wing' and 'too extremist' at the time. I had recently been to America and chattered a lot about a feminist revolutionary called Valerie Solanus who founded a group called SCUM – the Society for Cutting Up Men – and nominated Shulamith Firestone, another feminist firebrand and author of a book I much admired *The Dialectic of Sex: The Case for Feminist Revolution* (the revolutionary herself died a recluse and a pauper in 2012). The *Observer* likes to be left-wing in a nice, safe way. But I digress . . .

Circles of friends – and lovers – often turn out to have moved in interlocking circles, and my husband, Richard (always known in those days as 'Dick West') had also known Mary in the early 1960s. He actually shared living quarters with her, in a boarding house in Islington run by a very cordial woman who was a rich Trotskyist (as he recalled). One afternoon the doorbell rang and Dick, being in his digs at the time, answered it. It was Mary, who he recalled as a very shy and innocent young Irish girl, asking: 'Is the woman of the house at home?' And thus did she join the Islington *galere*. Dick even claimed to have 'politicised' Mary, with his talk of Tito and the Serbian Partisans, and his singing of the rousing anthems from the

Italian Communist Party (*'Avanti Populi! Alla riscosa! Bandiera Rossa Bandiera Rossa!'''* This merry song included, at the time, the words: 'Bandiera Rossa! Color di Vino! Viva Stalino! Viva Stalino!')

But if Mary was politicised in her early twenties, the seed sown didn't blossom until a little later. Her career at the *Observer* was successful, although not all her colleagues favoured her. The famous columnist Katharine Whitehorn thought Mary 'a pain in the neck'. Why so? 'She was so dismissive of motherhood and so negative about family life.'

There were romances, but they didn't work out, and Mary wasn't relaxed, at that time, about sexual matters. Perhaps that was the legacy of what she felt were her 'cauterised' emotions. But nearing her thirtieth birthday, she married the diplomat Ronald Higgins, in April 1966. It really was rather grand and the wedding reception was held in the crypt of the House of Commons, with Ted Heath as a guest of honour. There is a gorgeously chic photograph of Mary as a bride, not in white, but in a heavenly designer ensemble and a sweet Jackie Kennedy pillbox hat. Ron Higgins was mad about Mary, but the marriage would not work out.

The couple were posted to Indonesia by the British Foreign Office in 1966, just as the Vietnam war was reaching a crescendo. Mary was instructed by the F.O. never to speak about politics, but to concentrate on 'flowers and holidays' in her social conversation. Dick visited her in Indonesia when he was en route to Saigon, and she was consumed with envy that he was going into a war zone.

She found the role of a diplomatic wife maddeningly frustrating. It may be suggested that a union between a diplomat and a journalist is likely to be a mismatch: a diplomat is paid to keep secrets – 'to go abroad to lie for his country', was the old adage – while a journalist's instincts are to disclose information, especially that which is hidden from view. Her only real companion was a manservant called Joseph, with whom she felt she could actually talk politics.

Finally she fled back to London. Bernard Levin, a friend from her Fleet Street days, met her at London Airport with an armful of roses and a limousine. She burst into tears, just to be back to a life not controlled by Her Majesty's Diplomatic Corps. Ronald Higgins, who adored Mary, quit his Foreign Office job in an effort to win her back, but to no avail. Ron was in

many ways a domesticated man, which is something that feminists are supposed to like, but it ain't necessarily so. The marriage had been short
indeed, and Mary sought to return to her spiritual home, the *Observer*. In
1968, prompted by the liberal, but patrician editor David Astor (he was so
upper-class he once had to ask a member of his staff what a mortgage was),
Mary went to Northern Ireland and found the cause that was to dominate,
and perhaps to inspire, the rest of her life.

Her Irish roots were awakened – her parents, though servants of the
Crown had been Home Rule Irish nationalists – and her sense of justice
aroused by the situation she found. She became a superb reporter, and each
week her by-line on the *Observer* grew in authority. In 1970, she won the
International Journalist of the Year award from the International Press
Corporation for her reporting from, what she herself would always call 'the
North' (but which the International Press Corportion called 'Ulster').

Mary also fell in love with Eamonn McCann, the civil rights activist,
and this too was a true commitment of the heart. They were to live
together for some years and had a daughter and a son. They seemed a pas-
sionately romantic couple, and a beautiful couple too, walking up Grafton
Street, she in a tastefully hippyish coat of Indian design, he so tousle-
headed and merry and free. Their favourite love-song – a mournful one,
like all love-songs – was 'Peggy Gordon':

> *Oh, Peggy Gordon, you are my darling/ Come sit ye down upon my
> knee/ And tell to me the very reason/Why I am slighted so by thee.*

Mary worked at the *Observer* from 1968 to 1974, being based in
London. A moment of acrimony arose in 1974 when she was fired by
Conor Cruise O'Brien, then editor-in-chief, who felt that her reportage
was too biased towards Irish nationalism. Cruise O'Brien was coming to
feel that Sinn Féin/IRA was poisoning the waters of Irish cultural life, and
he developed a tremendous influence on Irish intellectuals throughout the
1970s and 1980s.

Conor had a lacerating phrase for those Irish people who were complacent about the bombings and killings carried out by the Provisional IRA
during these decades: 'the sneaking regarders'. Conor was courageous and
he acted as a corrective to those who were complacent about how much
bombs and bullets hurt. But Mary Holland's friends and colleagues were

outraged by this episode: Mary was certainly sympathetic to the Nationalist cause, – let's not call it the 'Catholic' cause, about which she would be more sceptical – and she was always committed to a united Ireland, but she was a conscientious person who cared about justice. After Conor Cruise O'Brien's departure from the *Observer*, Mary returned as a columnist.

However, she was ever more drawn to living in Ireland. She parted from Eamonn McCann in the late 1970s – they were, she said, fundamentally incompatible – and that included politics ('I'm basically a liberal', she said, whereas Eamonn really was a socialist, and indeed, a Trotskyist). Moreover he was not, in those days, one of nature's monogamists. And so she went to live in Dublin, selling up in Islington, which had become her home location in London, and finding a delightful old house, which looked liked a country rectory, in the Rathmines/Rathgar area.

Besides her work for the *Observer*, Mary became an influential columnist for the *Irish Times*. She also fronted, with Peter Jay, the politics programme *Weekend World* for London Weekend Television. Among her colleagues there was Peter Mandelson, with whom she stayed friendly. She co-founded, with Vincent Browne, *Magill* magazine, published in Dublin. In 1980, her television documentary *Creggan*, an account of life on a working-class estate in Derry, won the Prix Italia and British Broadcasting Guild award. In 1989 she shared, with David McKittrick of the London *Independent*, the Christopher Ewart-Biggs Memorial Prize for her contribution to better Anglo-Irish understanding. Among other awards, she was voted, in 1990, 'Cork Woman of the Year', in which she was hailed 'an illustrious daughter of west Cork'. This pleased her hugely.

Mary was also involved with feminist issues, and there was a moment when Dick West and I were in her Islington home and Mary and myself began stapling together a feminist newsletter. We were up against a deadline and Mary and I pleaded with Dick to help us: we were kneeling on the floor with pages from the newsletter all around. He resolutely refused.

After all his talk about Tito's Partisans, I'd have thought he'd have been ready to lend a hand. But Mary said, merrily but shrewdly, 'perhaps he feels that to be stapling feminists leaflets together is just sinking too low'. Mary went on to campaign for abortion rights before the controversial abortion referendum in Ireland in 1983. It was an issue on which we parted company, as I was researching a book about abortion, and I had forced myself to watch abortions at every stage of the procedure, and I found the operation gruesome and nightmarish.

But Mary was seldom personally argumentative – she had an innate sense of values and she felt, or came to feel, and I endorse the view, that friendship is more important than differing views on any subject, however fundamental. Mary was also an active trade unionist, which didn't interest me greatly – the only trade unions I had known in Fleet Street were deeply corrupt, though in time I came to see that this is part of the human condition, rather than necessarily part of the trade unions.

But the cause of Northern Ireland was always the priority, and she predicted, long before it occurred, or that anyone would even imagine that it might occur, that one day, Dr Ian Paisley would come to the conference table with Sinn Féin.

The last years of Mary's life were blighted by a degenerative illness, scleroderma, which started with an apparent case of poor circulation. It was a painful illness, which she accepted with a mixture of stoicism and ascerbic wit. Mary had a cutting side to her temperament: she could freeze with an ice-cold remark. But she was warm of heart, kind, decent and honourable.

Mary Holland died in St Vincent's Hospital, Dublin, a few days short of her sixty-eighth birthday, in 2004. Her last days were agonising – Nell McCafferty, an old and dear friend from Derry, who was with Mary towards the end was much distressed by her sufferings. I had visited her in her last months at Harold's Cross hospice, where she lay in bed like a small paper doll. We spoke of old times, a little, and she was greatly comforted by the birth of a granddaughter.

A circle of friends came to take her out, in as much as she could go out. She was not a believing Catholic, though she had been married in church, and she retained a certain affection for the faith symbols of her childhood: she was strangely comforted by the presence of an image of the Sacred Heart in that hospice. She also fretted that 'he doesn't have his Votive Light'. The picture had no such candle-light in front of it, and the Votive Light before the image of the Sacred Heart would have been a fixed aspect of her childhood. She mentioned this each time I visited.

She spoke warmly about Dick, who by 2004, was in declining health himself, and I needed to look after him ever more, as I recount elsewhere. 'Dick West got the right woman,' she said, with that half-sardonic sweet smile. 'The convent girl will do her duty! He's the lucky man!'

She was terrifically loyal, and deployed loyalty with wit. One summer of 1993, she and I shared a summer cottage at Lisdoonvarna, County Clare, to attend the Merriman Summer School. An old friend of hers, the left-wing writer Michael Farrell sidled up to her at the pub one evening and said: 'Aren't you concerned for your political reputation – sharing a house with a notorious right-winger like Mary Kenny?'

Rapidly she replied: 'And what about poor Mary Kenny's reputation – sharing a house with a notorious left-wing subversive like me?'

Mary was survived by her daughter, Kitty – who became an outstanding reporter herself - and granddaughter Rosie, her son Luke, and by the friendship of her former partner Eamonn McCann, her two brothers having predeceased her. After her death, the *Irish Times* published a collection of her articles, *How Far We Have Travelled – The Voice of Mary Holland*, (Edited by Mary Maher: Dublin, 2004).

I regretted that she hadn't attempted an autobiography, as her life was a fascinating saga of adventure and a beacon of our times. But I think she felt too 'cauterised', emotionally, to open all that up, and in my own sunset years, I can identify with that.

Mary Cummins
From Ballybunion to the Ballybunion Mary Cummins Media Weekend

Mary Holland, Mary Cummins and myself used regularly to have what we called a 'Three-Mary' lunch at Bernardo's restaurant, in Lincoln Place (it was sited – alas, now gone - behind Trinity College fields) in Dublin. We often wanted Mary Maher, also from the *Irish Times*, to join us, but she was often away from Dublin when these occurred. It's significant though, that so many women of our generation were indeed called Mary, being an indication of the intensity of the Marian culture that Ireland was, and perhaps significant, too, that so many of us rebelled against the Marian template of womanhood and quiescent virtue.

Mary Cummins, a fiercely strong feminist writer from Ballybunion, County Kerry, died in 1999, in her mid-fifties – she never would reveal her exact age and at the time she died, her friends didn't actually know her age. Only after her death did it emerge that Mary was born in 1944. Mary had lung cancer, which almost certainly derived from her very copious cigarette habit. When she was first having treatment for the lung tumour at St James's hospital, I went to see her and asked her how the chemotherapy had proceeded. 'It was agonising,' she said. 'I couldn't have got through it without a cigarette.'

Her daughter Daisy was obliged to bring Mary armfuls of cigarette packets – to the cancer ward. Most, or many of us smoked in our prime, in my generation – although few of my contemporaries' deaths were smoking-related – but Mary Cummins was the most driven smoker I have ever encountered. Everyone has to have some means of letting off steam, and

Mary had overcome a serious drinking habit, which had it continued, would have been worse: in drink you may kill someone else, be it on the road or through some other accident. In smoking, you only harm yourself, for the most part.

Mary and I once added up the amount of liquor we imbibed in one day in 1970. It was deplorable – and shameless. She worked at the *Irish Times* while I was at the *Irish Press*. The two offices were in the centre of town, within easy rich of our favourite watering-holes, whither one could nip in and out of for brief refreshments.

We shared these stories when we got sober, which was a long struggle. Stories of drinking days are kind of uproarious, but kind of awful, told in retrospect. She once told me that she had driven from Ballybunion, her home town in County Kerry, to Dublin entirely in 'blackout'. (Blackout is when an alcoholic goes through a procedure on automatic pilot, but remembers nothing of it afterwards.) She'd call into pubs on the way, with an elaborate little story about this being her one and only drink. 'I've a long drive, so I'll just have the one.' I've done as bad myself: I once drank Ribena and vodka from a baby-bottle with a friend at the wheel doing likewise, and we had a real baby – mine – in the back of the vehicle. Yes, I should have been arrested, but I did pay the price in nightmares of guilt afterwards.

Mary was the daughter of a garda – her father was William Cummins, the sergeant at Ballybunion. Her mother, Sheila, was from County Cork. Mary was the second of five children.

Mary's father loomed large in her life. I gathered that he was stern and piquantly, his strong principles were applied to observing the law about intoxicating liquor. He would, Mary told me, insist that licensed premises would shut down at 10.30 PM, as the law stipulated (10 PM on Sundays, and previously, 8 PM). More indulgent gardaí would turn a blind eye – up to a reasonable point – especially during the summertime, when the holiday season was in full swing. The pub landlords needed to make the best of that short vacation time. Sergeant Cummins took the view – generally more characteristic of the English than the Irish – that the law was the law and must be respected: and this, Mary suggested, made him unpopular in the town, particularly among traders.

Nevertheless, she learned how to be a journalist from her father. When she was a small child, he would take her for walks around the town and describe the terrain and the people. There was nothing he didn't know about the locality he policed. He also knew where there were 'problem' families, and what occurred. What a superb local policeman he must have been – modern life certainly feels the lack of a neighbourhood officer who knows every inch of his territory. The experience gave Mary a great grounding in reportage: there is nothing like being there, walking around the location, observing the people and knowing what is going on. This cannot be replaced by a trawl through Wikipedia.

Mary was also encouraged in her writing skills at her local school, St Joseph's in Ballybunion. Like other convent girls (I seem to be the sole exception, I add chippily), the nuns rewarded and encouraged her essay-writing. Her first job was in the civil service but she subsequently went to Wales where she trained as a nurse. As her elder sister Kathleen told me proudly, Mary won a 'Nurse of the Year' award in Wales. She qualified as a midwife at the respected Rotunda Hospital in Dublin – and again, her nursing career provided her with another helpful background in journalism. It made her knowledgeable about medical matters, and she had seen real life in hospital wards.

She always wanted to write, and she was helped into journalism by a man who was himself a metaphorical midwife to so many women as journalists – Donal Foley. Donal Foley was a remarkable man – a hugely jovial, clever, shrewd, and generous deputy editor at the *Irish Times*. It is widely acknowledged that he should have been appointed editor after the retirement of Douglas Gageby, but the *Irish Times* was not yet ready for a Catholic, and Donal was passed over for another candidate (a nice man, a diligent journalist, but a hopeless editor) who was in the Church of Ireland tradition.

Donal was a major player in the development of the *Irish Times* in general – he saw that it had the potential to expand its base to a rising Catholic middle class – and to the advancement of women in particular. He hired and encouraged so many women writers, including Maeve Binchy, Mary Maher, Nell McCafferty, Elgie Gillespie, Renagh Holohan, Theodora Fitzgibbon and indeed many more. He was a picker of talent, and understood that writers often need mentoring – and then a light hand on the tiller. He was marvellous to Mary Cummins, as to so many others (he even was encouraging to me, when I was working for a rival paper). Donal Foley (1921-88) is listed in the Royal Irish Academy's Dictionary of Biography.

Mary made her mark on the *Irish Times* in reportage, and, increasingly in her commitment to feminism, which was, or became, fiery and fervent. She also had a passionate romance with a colleague, now dead. He was married, and the advance of promising young women journalists was not appreciated by the fellow's wife (and not always by Donal's wife, either). But looking back, I think we were, as young women, pretty amoral about all these issues. We had the arrogance of youth. We did whatever we wanted to do. I think we regarded married men as 'fair game' – if they wanted to get involved, that was their choice. And anyway, wasn't this what 'liberation' was all about? If it feels good, do it!

The romance broke up, and in painful circumstances. I don't know when Mary's drinking became problematic but it was probably around the same time as mine did – in the mid-thirties. When you're young, you can punish your body to an extraordinary degree. The body begins to show the punishment at around the same time men stop being able to play good rugby – mid-thirties. Mary worked in London for a while, but after another crisis, she sought help, and once she entered into a programme of sobriety, she never touched another alcoholic drink. Her daughter Daisy was born in London, and Daisy became the central focus of Mary's life.

In her *Irish Times* column 'About Women' Mary had some of the most uncompromising feminist opinions I've encountered. And she sometimes sounded like a real man-hater. I once brought up the subject of men being killed in warfare – my late sister had a special sympathy for the sufferings of soldiers. But Mary said, with half a laugh: 'Who cares? They're only men!' Mary was a redhead, with sharp eyes and a gurgling laugh, and she had something of the fiery nature ascribed to the redhead.

And yet, while she had strong polemical views when writing a column, she brought to her reportage an honesty about drawing on the evidence. There was a divorce referendum proposed in Ireland in 1986, and Mary did some research in rural Ireland before writing about attitudes to divorce. Her understanding of the economic facts of life among small farmers was equally fiercely honest. 'You *can't* split up a thirty-acre farm,' she told me. (This reminded me of John Healy's trenchant autobiography *Nineteen Acres*, which explains with such insight just why the Irish peasant was so cautious about marriage in the first place.) She also clocked that women's property rights were just not sufficiently well established to ensure that divorce would work out fairly. Farmers' wives could be left without a roof over their head.

Mary grasped the point that real life experience is different from aspirational political demands. She supported abortion rights, and described a – slightly flakey – guy we both knew as 'really decent at heart – he's the kind of person who would always lend you money for any emergency or an abortion'. And yet, she also remarked to me: 'Abortion takes away from a woman.'

She developed lung cancer in 1996, and faced it with the an almost laughing bravery. She died, quite suddenly – we had thought she was in remission – in November 1999 and is buried in a windswept churchyard just outside Ballybunion.

I think Mary really wanted to be a novelist – she was an avid reader of fiction, and a fan of crime fiction – but perhaps her attitude was an illumination of the saying: 'the best is the enemy of the good.' Her standards were so high that they inhibited her from writing anything that would not meet those high standards.

Yet her ambition was, in a way, brought to fruition by her daughter, Daisy, who flourished first in the film business and subsequently as a novelist, Abby Green, and is altogether a credit to her mother, who bravely raised Daisy alone. Mary's father never did get to know that Mary had borne a child, although Sheila, her own mother, was most supportive and was a wonderful grandmother to Daisy.

As a child, Mary had been especially attached to her mother, who, not unlike some other Irishwomen of her generation, had spent time in America, where she had developed her education at night school. Sheila had something of the polish that a sojourn abroad often brings. There was also ambition there, which Mary must have drawn on. I got to know much more of Ballybunion after Mary's death, and was more drawn into the community there because of having been Mary Cummins' friend. I was delighted to be among those who opened the first Women in Media weekend in Ballybunion in April 2013, which was dedicated primarily to Mary Cummins, and which instigated the Mary Cummins Award for Women of Outstanding Achievement in the Media, awarded to the renowned television and radio journalist Miriam O'Callaghan.

Mary would indeed have been gratified that her name and reputation live on in her home town, though it is perhaps a sign of how the times have changed that it was a celebrity of the electronic media, not the written word which Mary so loved, who was laurelled with the first Mary Cummins Award.

June Levine

The contradictions of a sexual feminist

Some years ago, in the 1990s, I was approached by a relation of the late, iconic Irish folk singer Delia Murphy who asked me would I be interested in writing a biography of the great Delia.

I would indeed have been honoured to do so: Delia Murphy was adored in the 1940s and 1950s, and, heroically, she privately helped Jews to safety in Rome during the Second World War – her husband was the Irish Ambassador there. (She was formally reprimanded by an Irish civil servant for breaching neutrality, and the legend is that she replied spiritedly – 'Feck neutrality! Humanity is more important!') A throaty, passionate folk singer who had more in common with the Portuguese fado than with the lighter balladeers of the Irish genre, Delia was not fashionable in her time, although she was loved by those who followed her. In the Ireland of the 1940s and '50s, Frank Sinatra, Bing Crosby and the Big Band sound were the vogue. I like writing about those who weren't fashionable in their time, so the project attracted me for many reasons.

However, there were certain obstacles. No family papers were available, which drains a biography of human context. And secondly, it was suggested that my friendship with June Levine was not welcomed by the Murphy family: indeed, I was made to understand quite clearly that June Levine was seen as a marriage-wrecker and a home-breaker. If I were to write a biography of Delia Murphy, I should cease to be friendly with June Levine.

One of Delia Murphy's daughters had been married to Dr Ivor Browne, and Dr Browne had left his wife when he fell in love with June.

The wife saw herself as abandoned, and forced into a divorce which she would not have chosen. (There were also four children.) 'He preferred the sexual witchcraft of Miss Levine to his marriage,' I was told, not without some acrimony.

Nuala Fennell had said, at the time that this occurred, that it was a sad story. She had had many dealings, in her political career, with women who were classified as 'deserted wives', a category which, at the time, was regarded with sympathy and pity, and, indeed, as victims of injustice. 'And yet,' said Nuala, with equal compassion, 'who are we to judge? If a couple find a happiness together which has previously eluded them, is it our place to disapprove?' No, it is certainly not. But the spouse who feels herself to be the victim of divorce or abandonment is entitled to feel aggrieved, and to articulate those feelings.

And June, in her prime, was as alluring as a Lorelei: she was a raven-haired, blue-eyed, voluptuous woman with a fabulous figure – feminine, fashion-conscious, a lively conversationalist with a merry laugh. She was also a sensationally good cook. And predictably terrifically attractive to men. She once made a play for my late brother Carlos, who found her very nearly irresistible. It began when June asked him to adjust her bra-straps in the offices of *Creation* magazine, wriggling exquisitely in a tight Lane Turner sweater, and nearly got to the point of seduction when she invited him to her flat, late one night, emphasising the bottles of whiskey within (to which he was partial).

He desisted, since he was married by then, but he often spoke, with comic faux-agony about the struggle he underwent. June, he said, was gorgeous: all woman! (He also had a theory, and a not unusual one, that Jewish women were sexier; you could see that by their attitude to food.)

By Jewish rules, June wasn't actually Jewish, since her mother was Catholic, but the paternal Jewish side of her inheritance mattered to her just the same. She was born in December 1931 to teenage parents – her mother was only fifteen, her father seventeen – in a Romeo-and-Juliet Jewish-Catholic romance. Her mother was Muriel McMahon from a County Clare family, who was smitten with a Jewish boy whose parents had fled from Latvia, They married secretly at a Catholic church in

Marlborough Street, Dublin, on Yom Kippur, when the Jewish branch of the family was at synagogue.

They had five children – of whom June was the eldest – and despite the disparate backgrounds and teenage wedding, remained happily married all their lives. Although June herself always said that a fifteen-year gap between mother and daughter is way too short: she would have preferred a mother who was distinctly of a different generation.

June was baptised a Catholic, but went to a Jewish School in Dublin – Zion. In 1947 the whole family converted to Judaism. It was a strangely smooth transfer, and all her life June retained both a strong sense of Jewish tradition, and a special affinity for the Blessed Virgin. In later years, June became attached to India, telling me – 'you don't know what spirituality is until you have experienced India.'

She got a job as a very young reporter on the *Irish Times* – when she was just fifteen. But love intervened when she fell for a young Canadian medical student at the Dublin College of Surgeons, Ken Mesbur. When he qualified, the couple, and their two young children migrated to Canada. In the small town of Arcona, Ontario, where they settled, a third baby was born. Arcona was a town of about 500 people, and gradually, June came to feel she was being buried alive: there was no outlet for her creativity, ambition or ideas.

June embodied a spirit stirring among women at that time, and articulately expressed by Betty Friedan's book, *The Feminine Mystique*. Friedan charted the life of the restless, intelligent wife, cooped up in suburban boredom, asking the existential question: 'Is this all there is?'

The situation drove June into a serious depression, and she fled back to Dublin, with her three children. She had a mental breakdown. The marriage was over.

Emerging from this crisis, she began to re-enter journalism at a time in the 1960s when opportunities were starting to open up. She worked for *Creation* magazine, for *Image*, and when I first met her in 1968, she was editing a magazine, the *Irishwomen's Journal*. Though June had written about fashion – and struck up a close friendship with Terry Keane, which, despite tiffs and differences, lasted until the end of their lives – she felt increasingly attracted to campaigning feminism. Thus she came to be part of the founding group of the Irish Women's Liberation Movement in 1970-71.

June was part of the famous 'condom train' – she alleged (which I contested) that she had been put in charge of me, so that I wouldn't run too wild on the excursion. Yet her interests were a lot wider than contraceptive freedom. She knew what it was like to be a single mother, and she was concerned for the victims of what she saw as a patriarchal society. Her father, though much-loved in the family, had been a conventional man who thought a woman's place was in the kitchen.

June went on to write what is considered a standard text on the roots of the IWLM, *Sisters*: although I must own I didn't always see eye-to-eye with her view of the movement, or the personalities involved. But that is normal: we all have our own view of a narrative, and as Carlyle wrote of the death of Louis XVI: ten thousand witnesses will tell ten thousand stories of the event.

Her personal life went through stages of turbulence, but later in the 1970s, she met, and finally married, the psychiatrist Ivor Browne. With compelling honesty, he describes in his autobiography, *Music and Madness*, the painful circumstances in which he separated from his first wife Orla Murphy, and the anguish at being parted from his four children. He too had gone through a serious depression, but when he met June, he came to feel a sense of peace, and their union was lasting and devoted, despite the cost to which Ivor himself attests. She told me: 'The holes in my head fitted into the rocks in his.' Ivor always called her 'Juno', which reflected her mother-goddess status.

Like all of us, June contained many contradictions. She was a committed feminist, but she was also a man's woman: a crusader for women's rights to fulfillment outside the home, and yet, one of the most accomplished housewives I have ever known – her home was faultless, her table exquisite, her hostess abilities peerless.

She had worked as a researcher for Gay Byrne on the *Late Late Show*, but towards the end of her life she excoriated TV and all its malign works. She resolutely refused to have anything to do with TV documentaries which sought her co-operation, even about subjects that mattered to her.

June was in some ways a sexual liberal, in that she believed women

should be free to make their choices without stigma. Yet she retained elements of conservatism, both from Judaism and perhaps from nature. She
often cited what the Rabbi had taught her, about the need for respect, on
the eve of her first wedding: 'When you approach one another as a married
couple, do so as if you were putting on your best dress.' She wrote about
having an abortion, and then waking up from the anaesthetic saying –
'Where's the baby?' She was a very maternal woman, and adored her children and grandchildren, which included a step-grandchild who was as
dear to her as the rest of the family.

Later in life (like many of us, again) June became more of a sexual puri-
tan – anyway, an element of puritanism is never far from feminism
(remember Christabel Pankhurst's immortal cries of 'Votes for Women –
And Chastity for Men!') After her experience of writing *Lyn* – the story of
a Dublin woman horribly victimised by prostitution – she became vehe-
mently, even fanatically convinced that prostitution should be banned, and
that any man found to be involved with it should be prosecuted, as in
Sweden. Conversation on this subject became almost fanatical, and certainly irrational: prostitution is lowering, and particularly revolting when
it involves young women who are coerced or trafficked, but prohibiting it
is unrealistic – and the Swedish state is often far too controlling of the personal lives of its citizens.

June suffered a series of strokes in her last year when her speech was
affected, and I now wonder if she had had some mini-strokes previous to
the major episodes. She struggled courageously to regain her powers of
communication, and seemed to improve. But in the first week of October
2010, there was another serious stroke: she lost consciousness and passed
away peacefully in the early hours of 14 October. She was much mourned
by a wide circle of family and friends: her daughter Diane, her sons Adam
and Michael, and their spouses, her three grandchildren and one step-
grandchild.

June Levine will have her place in Irish social history as an inspiring
feminist, and whenever the Irish Women's Liberation Movement is mentioned, so is June. But for all that, and for all her stunning looks and sex-
appeal, the home and the family remained at the heart of her most
passionate attachments.

I had much affection for June, although I had differences with her too, and we had some lively debates. Yet I was always beguiled by her kindness, and my Dublin flat is full of thoughtful gifts that she generously bestowed on me.

Because of the conditions implied – to break with June – I never did proceed with the plan to write a biography of Delia Murphy. Another writer, Aidan O'Hara, produced a very pleasing text and I wrote an introduction. We make choices: we can never go back on them.

Clare Boylan
From journalist to literary novelist

Clare Boylan was a beauty – she looked like a sweet and adorable flapper from the 1920s – as well as a writer of international literary repute. She was only fifty-eight years of age when she died of ovarian cancer in May 2006. Even when she was in her last days, at the Harold's Cross hospice in Dublin, she was exquisitely presented, so fastidious in her appearance and utterly brave. The perfectly applied make-up could not quite disguise the ravages that cancer inflicts on a thinning face and transparent bone structure, and yet, she still looked pretty.

I am not good at dealing with death directly: my inclination is to play-act and pretend it isn't happening. Clare played along with this too:.We knew, perhaps, it was the last conversation, but her tone was cool and philosophical. She reflected on aspects of life almost cheerfully, and I think with resignation. She did say she didn't care a bit if she never wrote another word, which was strangely comforting.

My great fear is that I will die before I have written what I need to write, and compassionately, Clare said – 'that's a terrible thing to fear.' She understood all the fears of a writer, and was a great teacher and tutor to writers.

When we parted she hugged me closely. I still pretended to myself that I would see her again.

Clare was the friend of my youth: once, back in the 1960s, we sat up all night writing a play together, to submit it for a drama competition for RTÉ. We got a great sense of achievement from doing it, though the play didn't get anywhere. It is still somewhere in my archives, a curio of past times and girlhood aspirations.

Clare was the youngest of three girls, of an equally beautiful mother whom they all adored, and a civil servant father who was odd at the best of times, but became quite dangerous with Alzheimer's (she wrote about this in her novel, based on fact, *Beloved Stranger*). The family grew up in modest circumstances in Rathmines, Dublin, charmingly chronicled in her book *Rome for a Single Lady*.

Her mother, Evelyn, had also been a writer and Clare's ambition was to be a more successful writer, an ambition encouraged and advanced by her mother – it has been observed that many of the themes in her fiction are about mothers and daughters. She was ambitious from the start of her career with the Dublin *Evening Press* (she started working straight after school – there was neither opportunity, nor, I think interest on her part, to go to university. People impatient to achieve in life just want to get on with it: university may defer that course of direct action.)

She had been gifted from childhood,winning a children's art award, as well as a poetry prize. As a young reporter she was awarded a Journalist of the Year accolade for reportage. She enjoyed journalism but she really wanted to develop into literary fiction, which she did with her first book, *Holy Pictures*, published to acclaim in 1983.

Clare had a kind of steely, but joyous, femininity: loved fashion, dressed like a 1920s model, idolised Colette, and Charlotte Brontë, whose unfinished novel became Clare's most renowned work, *Emma Brown*, published on both sides of the Atlantic in 2003. She edited the fashion and lifestyle magazine, *Image*, with brio. Clare always combined journalism with literary work, and managed her time very efficiently. If she was writing a book and needed money, she'd turn to journalism – that's what journalism was for: earning money! As in everything else, Clare was successful as a journalist, and enjoyed contributing to the *Guardian*. She also enjoyed a harmlessly flirtatious lunch with the *Guardian* editor, Alan Rusbridger.

I was initially (and naively) shocked when she said that she regarded journalism as inferior to literary writing: she described journalism as 'practising scales' before settling down to real piano-playing – literary writing. I always thought that journalism wouldn't work unless you gave it your all; later I came to feel I gave it too much of my all, and the yellowing cuttings of old newspapers mean little with the passage of time.

But she taught me a lot about writing – I, who was initially a successful journalist, yet slow to find my voice, I feel, as a writer. She taught me to take it professionally and to stand up for my own work. She believed writers should not be shy about money. She believed writers should sometimes be tough. She was personally generous, and even occasionally vague about money, but she was fierce in her views that writers should be paid, and that they should be properly paid, and feel confident about asking to be paid.

She developed this sense of affirmation about just wages early in life: as a teenager, she and her sisters, Ann and Patricia, had a singing group, The Girlfriends. They were invited by a seasoned performer, Hal Roach, to do a spot at the Apollo, Walkinstown, being promised thirty shillings (now translated at £1.50, but in the early 1960s it might be half a week's wages for a junior shorthand typist) for the gig. At the end of the evening, performance given, there was no cash forthcoming. Clare threatened to seize the microphone and expose Roach for his parsimony to his adoring fans, whereupon he produced a ten-shilling note for her. (Her sisters, not so bold, never received their promised ten bob.)

Clare married young – she was the first contemporary of mine to get married. She did not have children, simply because 'it didn't turn out that way'. She had a sane attitude to motherhood: she would have accepted a child with pleasure, interest and curiosity, she told me. But she would not be fretful or neurotic if she didn't have a baby, and she wasn't. Though she wrote about children better than any author I can think of, capturing their thinking and conversation unnervingly well.

We once had a conversation on the sensitive issue of perhaps having a handicapped child, which arose from, I think, an article about the amniocentesis which could predict whether an unborn child might be affected by a disability.

Clare said, perhaps unexpectedly, that she wouldn't wish to terminate a pregnancy in such circumstances. This wasn't an attitude formed from a particularly religious standpoint but because, she said, she felt she would have grown too attached to the child. A humane and honest avowal, and a fresh way of regarding a painful dilemma.

She believed in being affirmative and confident as a woman, and she was supportive of women's rights – she felt that her mother had not had sufficient opportunities for her talents – but she had scant interest in feminism as a political ideology. Rightly, I think, she knew that a true writer cannot have too many distractions, and that political activity subtracts from the energy of writing work. Clare would not, either, have been in sympathy with moaning about 'patriarchy', nor the more extreme complaints about 'sexual harassment'. Clare had a sense of humour, and a sense of appreciation of the humorous interplay, banter and flirtatious exchanges between men and women.

One day she was complaining about some editorial issue to Donal Foley of the *Irish Times*. They were having a drink in a pub in Duke Street, just off Dawson Street. In response to Clare's discourse, Donal looked down at her open-toed sandals and said: 'Haven't you a lovely pair of little feet!' Clare laughed merrily at that and recalled it in merriment, too. She didn't think it was patronising; she thought it was charming and refreshingly unexpected. She did have sweet little feet too: she was petite and dainty in stature and bearing.

Clare loved cats (and authored *The Literary Companion to Cats*) with their grace, and their independence. And she was another of my friends who was an outstanding cook (among my contemporaries in Dublin I knew four women who were amazingly gifted cooks – without, it almost seemed, making any fuss about it at all: Mavis Arnold, Clare Boylan, Noeleen Dowling and June Levine) and I remember many delicious dinner parties in her County Wicklow home with her husband, Alan Wilkes – sharp-eyed, witty, caustic.

She wrote seven novels, three short story collections and authored two anthologies about the writers' craft, as well as teaching and tutoring in creative writing. She had always been fascinated by Charlotte Brontë, and her last book, Emma Brown was a completion of an unfinished novel by Brontë. She put a huge amount of research into it, and it was a literary triumph, and it was purchased by an American publisher for a handsome sum, and highly praised in the prestigious *New York Review of Books*.

Clare always worried about her husband, Alan's health because he had had a brush with heart problems in middle life, while Clare herself was the picture of health. But on the evening of the launch of *Emma Brown* in Soho, her brow was furrowed with a pain she could not quite conceal. She had complained of back pain for a while, and when driving, she needed to bolster the small of her back with soft cushions. Yet it was so unexpected when she was diagnosed with ovarian cancer. Her attitude was characteristically philosophical: some people say 'Why me?' she reflected. Her response was: 'Why not me?'

She had treatment, including radical surgery, and was able to spend some time in a house she and Alan had acquired in Brittany. But after a remission, the cancer returned. In the last month of her life, her friend – and indeed mine – Noeleen Dowling nursed Clare with utter devotion, as did Alan. It is such a privilege to have the care of friends as life recedes: Clare deserved it.

I don't think I ever discussed faith issues with Clare: she had been to convent school, with the St Louis nuns (who had the reputation of being hard taskmistresses), but she was neither markedly devotional nor markedly disparaging of religious issues. Clare saw the quirky in life, rather than the polemical and she accepted traditional rituals as part of the land scape and culture of our lives. She had grown up in a street with several Jewish families, where the Catholic children used to run errands for Jewish neighbours during Jewish holidays (when Orthodox Jews were forbidden to participate in practical tasks) and that gave her an affection and an insight for Jewish life.

She was also brought up with the rules of honesty that most of our families shared: she and her sister once found a ten-shilling note on the street in Terenure, and were instructed by their parents to hand it in at the Garda station. They did so, and the Gardaí told them that if it went unclaimed for a year and a day, they could have it for themselves. A year and a day later, they were given their reward, for honesty and for patience. Dear Clare: you won't be forgotten, and sometimes I still can't believe you've gone from this world.

Maeve Binchy
From talented reporter to a world brand

Many's the gin and tonic I lifted with dear Maeve Binchy – when we were both young journalists – usually at the Pearl Bar, that Dublin watering-hole now, alas, no more. We even once invented a diet together – the grapefruit-and-gin-and-tonic diet, which consisted of eating nothing but grapefruit, and drinking nothing but gin (large) and tonic (diet). We ended up very drunk with a lot of citrus acid in our stomachs. Yet Maeve could hold her liquor: she was over six foot tall (which made her a schoolgirl netball ace), and, as an adult never less than fourteen stone in weight, and that body mass means much fortitude when it comes to imbibing, and absorbing, alcohol.

Maeve was always worried – and sensitive – about her weight: she had tipped the scales at fifteen stone even as a schoolgirl, and I was always fighting the flab, so we were both obsessed about diets, as young women. But in a roundabout way, it was Maeve's weight worry which made her a storyteller. At school – the enlightened Holy Child convent in Killiney – she became the class entertainer, the narrator of funny stories possibly as a compensation for her burgeoning weight. She wouldn't be the prettiest girl in the class, but she would be the funniest, the cleverest at beguiling people with her dazzling conversation and her way with stories. Maeve was often amusing and self-deprecating about her weight, but she was also sensitive about it, and thought those who made fun of fat people were cruel. The only short story she ever wrote which had a strong theme of vengefulness was about a woman on board a ship who was horrible to the overweight.

I always thought Maeve was an amazingly good reporter – sharp as a tack, an acute observer of people and events. Her report of Princess Anne's wedding to Mark Phillips in 1973 was hilarious, although some readers thought it so critical and sharp that there were letters saying she should be renamed 'Maeve Bitchy'. She got shoals of mail and regretted afterwards that she didn't keep it in an archive. She told me in retrospect that she thought *Irish Times* readers remembered with fondness the stories about the King and Queen of England and the two little princesses, Elizabeth and Margaret Rose, being so brave during the Blitz, and they felt it was so unkind to have a go at the royals. Maeve was never unkind: she was a reporter with an observant edge, and an humorous eye which included a fitting sense of irreverence.

When Maeve began writing fiction, I was rather disappointed, because I valued her journalism, and I felt she was turning to a softer medium – I might even have considered the popular novel a soppier medium. But that was what she had always wanted to do, and she had loved to tell stories within the genre of reportage. She started with newspaper features, drawn on her experience of living in a kibbutz in Israel: there was a brilliant series over a Christmas holiday period called 'Women Are Fools' into which she wove human stories that she had experienced from the kibbutz. I admired the stories and the way she had chosen to do it. It was also unlikely that any Israelis would be reading the *Irish Times* so as to identify themselves in the accounts of disappointed love and emotional breakdown.

Maeve wrote about everyone she knew, she said. We were sitting in a Fleet Street restaurant one day called the Val Ceno (where you could order six bottles of wine in advance, to tide you over the pub-closing hours, in London, of 3 PM until 5 PM). There were four or five of us. 'You're in my books,' she told me. Then she went around the table. 'And so are you, and you, and you.' None of us recognised ourselves within the Binchy oeuvre.

Yet she never forsook journalism, and continued, almost to the end of her life writing for the *Irish Times*.

Maeve had, for a writer, a disadvantageous childhood: it was a supremely happy home in Dalkey, where she was the eldest of four. She loved her parents and adored her siblings. A friend of mine who read Edna O'Brien's memoir *Country Girl* said that what she really hated about Edna's story was the way she disparaged her parents. Maeve would never have done that. The story she told me about her parents was the way in which they sat up all night making a doll's house so that she should have it on Christmas morning. Neither did she have a repressed or wretched time at school. The nuns loved her too, and she visited some of them until they died. In Maeve's fictions, nuns are nearly always very nice, and indeed, priests are usually kindly characters as well.

Maeve was critical of Catholic Ireland, mainly I think, because she felt that the intensity of her faith collapsed into ashes when she was a young adult. She once said: 'I feel I've been sold a pup.' Her brother Billy said that he thought Maeve had lost her childhood faith, and never replaced it with an adult faith. Perhaps so. In any case she told the story often, and highly entertainingly, of how she lost her faith while in Israel.

It was arranged in the kibbutz that she would work on Saturdays, which was the Jewish Sabbath, and in return, she would have Sundays off, being the Christian version. One exceptionally hot Sunday she set off to find the location where it was said the Last Supper took place. She heaved herself up a mountainside – and in telling the story Maeve would act out the heat and the effort involved for a fifteen-stone woman to climb up a rocky mountain in such conditions. On the first ledge she encountered a holy man, who was sitting in rags and cross-legged, intoning and ululating some incomprehensible imprecation. More heaving herself up in the broiling heat, now thirsty and dusty. Finally she got to a desolate-looking cave, guarded by a Brooklyn-born Israeli soldier.

Maeve sat down on the rock, exhausted, and said: 'is that all it is?' The Israeli solder wisecracked back with New York wit: 'What'ya expect, Ma'am – a Renaissance table set for thirteen?'

Maeve burst into a torrent of tears and answered angrily, 'Yes, that's just what I did expect, if you want to know! But . . . none of it is true, is it? It's all just a fairytale!' And that, she maintained, was the moment she lost her faith. Her biographer, Piers Dudgeon, claims that she became an existentialist at UCD, and this contributed to her agnosticism, or atheism. She decided that we have to take control of our own lives and make our own choices, and not depend on being told some comforting story about everything coming right once we're in the next world.

She had, indeed, been very devout as a young girl and a teenager, and her saints were real people to her. But of course that too is an imaginative life which feeds the writer's sensibilities.

Maeve's home life was wonderful (although sadly, she lost her mother when Maureen was only fifty-seven), but because of her weight she always worried she wouldn't get a boyfriend, and had the experience that most of us have had: going to a teenage dance and not getting a single invitation to dance (all the more bitter as Maeve was a good dancer).

She got into journalism basically because her parents had so much confidence in her. She wrote such descriptive letters home from Israel that her father sent them to the *Irish Independent* and had them published. Which of our parents would have had the self-assurance to take such a course? Maeve's father was a distinguished lawyer, and her uncle a judge; they had the assurance of the upper-middle class although in those days lawyers weren't pulling in loads of money as they are today.

Maeve qualified as a teacher first, and did some teaching, and then moved on to travel journalism, which was again a great source of experience. And then she was hired by the *Irish Times*, by that duo of men who did so much for aspiring women writers – Douglas Gageby and Donal Foley. Maeve worked superbly well with Mary Maher on the *Irish Times*, and that was a lifetime friendship.

And what about boyfriends? She always was a woman who wanted love and commitment, and a sexually fulfilling relationship. There was at least one very unhappy love affair: her biographer, Piers Dudgeon, claims that she was made bitterly unhappy by being dumped by Jack MacGowran, the actor who did such distinguished work in the theatre with Beckett, and in the cinema with Polanski, but that was in London.

There was also a relationship in Dublin which went awry, and Maeve was seen in the Pearl Bar one evening in floods of tears. She was a vulnerable and sensitive person when it came to love. But Maeve was also a writer, and as Graham Greene has noted, every writer must have a chip of ice in his heart so as to stand back and coolly record every experience. As Dickens never forgot the humiliations of the blacking-factory so Maeve, I think, used what emotional pain she experienced in her work.

Her short stories contain many examples of women who are having affairs with married men which the reader knows will end in tears, while the character does not. In *The Lilac Bus*, one of the passengers is Dee, who is in the midst of an unhappy affair with a married man, a medical consultant called Sam Barry. Sam Barry's promises to divorce his Canadian wife are very evidently hollow, but Dee is so desperately in love with him that she cods herself it will be all right. (In the end, she summons up the courage to call it off.) Similarly, in one of her *Central Line* stories, 'Lancaster Gate', a nervous young woman, Lisa, checks into a London hotel with her married lover for a weekend. The sex is fine – he liked it, and that made Lisa happy – but there is always the anxiety about being discovered. When it emerges that her lover's wife is expecting another baby, Lisa is baffled: he had maintained he hadn't even seen his wife in the previous six months.

'Shepherd's Bush', too, features a young Irish woman, May, who has come to London to have an abortion because she's involved in a 'hopeless affair' with a married man in Dublin. May has no real qualms about seeking a termination – she just feels it's necessary since her lover will never leave his wife and four children. And, she reckons, 'the child that she was going to get rid of was still only a speck' – though she is discomforted by an Irish nurse at the clinic describing the continual practice of terminations as like working in 'a death factory'. However, May is cheered by her Australian roommate, Helen, who thinks having an abortion is a great lark and everyone should have one regularly – she upbraids May for not getting her lover to pay for the procedure. May hasn't even told the lover, let alone asked for money.

In 'Dinner in Donnybrook', in the collection *Dublin 4*, there's another drolly ironic story about a husband, a wife, a mistress, and a dinner-party at which no one is quite sure who knows what. 'Decision in Belfield' is another story in the collection with an abortion theme.

* * *

Maeve always wanted to have a happy marriage, and in her thirties, she achieved just that, when she married Gordon Snell, the children's writer who was also, in the 1970s, a presenter for BBC Radio 4. One night I met Maeve in a faintly disreputable pub in Fleet Street, and Dick ambled in. We talked about going on to dinner somewhere, and Maeve then said there was a very nice fellow at the BBC whom she knew, and maybe she'd call him and we'd make a foursome. And so Gordon joined us and he and Maeve quite literally lived happily ever after. She dedicated every book she every wrote to him.

She told her biographer that it was a sadness when she discovered, in her late thirties, that she couldn't have children. Looking back on our conversations, I am not entirely sure whether she wanted children, although she was always generous-spirited about friends' offspring, and was adorable about grandchildren (quoting Gore Vidal's sardonic 'Never have children, only have grandchildren'). In any case, Maeve was entirely happy just being married to Gordon.

Maeve was warm and generous, but behind all the hilarity of our Pearl Bar days, she was an organised and methodical person – the discipline of the teacher never left her. Maeve's was always the first Christmas card you received in the first week of December, because she had written them in October. She never really wasted time, and once she was set on the road to success with her fiction, she applied herself continuously to her work. In the end, she outsold every major Irish writer, from James Joyce to Edna O'Brien, and became a template for a generation of women writers who followed her.

When she produced her first book, *Light a Penny Candle*, the publishers were initially disappointed that there was no explicit sex in it, as there was a convention that there should be a sex scene every nineteen pages. Maeve said, truthfully, that as she hadn't lead a very colourful sex life, she wouldn't know how to write explicit sex scenes, and the publishers came to accept that. The book, of course, was a runaway success, on both sides of the Atlantic, and it showed that there is always a market for readers who don't want explicit sex in their stories, as well as those who do.

She told me about visiting some American mid-western town on a book tour where the ladies would approach her and say, 'Oh Miss Binchy, we're so grateful to have stories with no pornography and no profanity – I'll have four copies, two for my aunts, one for the pastor's wife and another for myself . . .' One of her greatest fans in America was Barbara Bush, Mrs George Bush Snr.

And yet she did write about sex, but she wrote it – and its problems as well as its pleasures – within the context of relationships, families, friends and communities. Some of her novels are also accurate social reflections of changing values in Ireland - *Tara Road*, for example, is a flawless tracking of property prices in the Dublin between the 1970s and the end of the century.

People loved – and love – Maeve's books because they are human and they are redemptive: the characters find answers to their problems, and help each other to work things out. They also reflected Maeve's warm and positive personality. Despite suffering a great deal of pain in later life, from arthritis, and discomfort from sleep apnea, she always found blessings to count: she always practised an attitude of gratitude.

Nobody is universally popular or liked by absolutely everyone. There were those who were critical. One mutual friend says: 'Maeve never took risks as a writer. And a writer should take risks. She stayed in the comfort zone.' Mary Cummins and Maeve were not always the best of buddies: Mary thought Maeve too people-pleasing – 'all that *plamas*' – and Maeve thought Mary 'difficult'.

Maeve would have identified herself as a feminist, but she never actually joined a feminist group. She wasn't politically engaged. But she possessed a quality which her women friends greatly envied: she could command men. Maeve was a brilliant conversationalist – one of the most accomplished I have ever heard (and I've known some, especially in Ireland), and she could hold a circle of male listeners spellbound, and then they'd be doubled-up laughing at her stories. Very few men, in the 1960s and 1970s, were so respectful of a woman's ability to talk – and very few women could command a barful, or roomful of competitive males in the way that Maeve could.

Maeve died in July 2012, and a nation mourned. Indeed, the world mourned, since it was world news. Her age was given as seventy-two, as her public date of birth was 1940. But Piers Dudgeon has subsequently revealed that she was born a year earlier – in 1939. She was a year older all her life than she was officially – likely to be an error of her mother's making rather than her own. It is the kind of vignette in a person's life from which Maeve herself would have crafted an explanatory story.

Part Four
Sexual Politics

When a Priest is Named as a Paedophile

We have all read accounts of offences by paedophile priests and asked ourselves 'how could it happen?' and 'how could they get away with it?' And 'what part of "it is wrong to have sex with children" do they not understand?' Yet the whole story takes on a more complex perspective when the scandal occurs close to home, and the person accused is a friend.

Father Kit Cunningham, a member of the Rosminian Order who died in Dublin in December 2010, aged seventy-nine, had been a friend of mine, and of my husband's, for more than thirty years. We were very fond of Kit, who was great company, gregarious, generous in spirit, a little too fond of the vino and the vodka, manifestly ecumenical, totally tolerant, and a benign flirt with the ladies. He had that unmistakable glint in his eye, of a man who likes women, and I can think of a dozen women who warmed to him, and half a dozen who were brought into the Catholic church by his evangelisation. He seemed to his friends to be a fine pastor at London's oldest Catholic church, St Etheldreda's – built in 1290 – in Ely Place, London EC1, near Fleet Street and perhaps in consequence to its proximity to newspaper life, Kit became unofficial chaplain to the print media. We all liked Kit, or so I thought.

Above all, Kit seemed kind. If St Etheldreda's was a hub for historians – Henry VIII gave the last supper there for his first wife, Catherine of Aragon and Kit still had the menu – as rector, Kit never overlooked the down-and-outs who would often knock on the door for help. He set up a special cafeteria to feed the needy. He was also on ecumenically good terms with the local Rabbi, who ministered to a congregation in Hatton Garden, a street specialising in diamond merchants and craftsmen, and the two would sometimes share transport when doing chaplain duties together at

Wormwood Scrubs prison. It was a standing joke between them that Kit's clients at the Scrubs – mostly Liverpool Irish – were usually doing time for grevious bodily harm, while the Jewish prisoners were usually arraigned for embezzlement or cooking the books: when the Jews go off the rails they do so with their brains, when the Liverpool Irish go awry they do so with their fisticuffs. (Kit was half-Irish, himself, on his father's side, as the Cunningham name implies. His mother was from a Lancashire Catholic family who had kept the old faith all during the Reformation and afterwards.)

And then, on 21 June 2011, a devastating documentary was shown on BBC 1 called *Abused: Breaking the Silence*, made by Olenka Frenkiel. In this documentary, it was alleged, with compelling witness statements, that as a priest in Africa in the 1960s, Kit Cunningham had sexually abused young boys at a boarding school, St Michael's, in Soni, Tanzania.

Kit Cunningham, the merry priest I had known for over three decades, was described in this television broadcast as 'a predatory paedophile' and a danger to young boys. John Poppleton, aged fifty-two at the time of interview, who had been a young boy at Soni, spoke about the horrific experience of being told to lower his pyjamas so that Kit could fondle him. 'He then pulled his pyjamas down, laid on his bed and made me [perform a sex act].' According to Mr Poppleton, this happened several times. Another former pupil said that he had been 'twisted forever' by the experience of this sexual abuse. Sam Simeonides, another victim, described Kit Cunningham as 'a monster'.

One of the victims said that 'pain, fear, assault, punctuated by caresses' was his experience of knowing Kit Cunningham as a young priest.

In 2009, the victims had got together via the Internet and sent their testimony to Father David Myers, the Provincial of the Rosminian Order in Britain. Kit, by now in retirement and in declining health, apparently acknowledged his guilt and asked the victims for forgiveness. A letter was shown on the programme in which he had written: 'I beg you to forgive me.' There were other clerical abusers in that boarding school – an isolated place in the middle of what was then Tanganyika – and Kit wrote in his letter that he 'should have done more to stop it.'

One boy, Don McFarlane, who had been sexually abused by another priest – Bill Jackson – was told, as a boy, by Kit that he would be in big trouble if he ever reported the abuse. 'Woe betide you, young man, if you ever say anything about this.' (These boys were usually between nine and eleven.) Not for the first time, it wasn't just the sexual abuse which distressed the victims – it was the covering up and the way in which they were bullied into silence.

Kit had been awarded the honour of an MBE for his services to the community in 1987 – he looked very fine in his top hat going off to Buckingham Palace to receive his award from the Queen – and now he was persuaded by a friend in Dublin, John Hughes (he had retired to Ireland by then) to return it as a gesture of penitence. This was March 2010. This showed not only moral penitence but implied legal liability, and the Rosminian Order was subsequently sued for compensation, and for covering up the assaults. The Order could well be bankrupted by the financial consequences: twenty-two out of thirty-five pupils are suing for compensation, and one of the victims, John Poppleton, says that if the order goes bankrupt as a consequence – 'I'd be happy' – because such a penalty would serve to protect children in the future from the torment that he and his colleagues had experienced at Soni.

* * *

We wonder why clerical abuse was 'covered up', as well as how it could have occurred. Now I have some insight into the answer. Because, at first, you just do not believe it. It can seem so utterly uncharacteristic of the person you knew. The whole picture seems uncharacteristic of the person you knew, and you wonder if monetary compensation, suggested by aggressive lawyers, may be the driving force of so many paedophile allegations. Where there is a supply of money, there will be a demand, and there is no scheme in this wide world, however well-intentioned, which has not been exploited as a racket.

However, this response is probably partly a defence mechanism, a psychological denial. There is at least one friend of Kit's – who shared living quarters with him for some years – who regards such paedophile claims as fantasy: 'it's like the witchhunts. If she sinks, she's a witch, if she floats, she's a witch. If he shows interest in children, he's a paedophile. If he shows no interest in children, he's a *cunning* paedophile.'

Although disbelieving at first, I came to accept that the evidence brought to light in the *Abused* documentary was altogether compelling, and true. As a young priest, in the middle of Africa, he clearly had sexually abused young boys. It didn't shock me, as if I were some Victorian maiden aunt appalled by the horrors of reality and the bestiality of men. I've seen enough of the world, and know enough about human nature, and about my own experiences, too, to understand that people are capable of bad and crazy actions that may seem well out of character, but it happens.

But perhaps I was shocked by my own misjudgement, and indeed that of my husband, Richard West, who loved Kit's company. Dick didn't, as a rule, much care for Catholic priests – he retained an Englishmen's prejudices against 'Arsees', as they used to be called when he did his National Service in the British Army. He was inclined to suggest that all 'Arsee' padres were Jesuitical clerics involved in some fiendish plot against the interests of England. When we were on what was laughably called our honeymoon (aren't all honeymoons mildly disastrous?) in Spain in 1974, I asked Dick if he had any spare Spanish pesetas when I was popping into a church. 'Why give them money?' he said, only half-joking. 'They'll only spend it on more torture instruments.'

And yet Kit Cunningham dissolved all of Richard's prejudices against Catholic priests. Kit was so different from any he had met previously. They talked together about Chesterton and Dr Johnson and chortled over their common favourite Dickens volume, *The Pickwick Papers*, (a closed book to me). They talked a lot, too, about Africa, since Dick had reported many times from Africa and had written books about South Africa, the Congo, and Liberia: one of his books on South Africa, *The White Tribes of Africa*, had a mildly iconic status among the aforesaid white African tribes of English-speakers and Afrikaners.

Africa inspires affection but also exasperation in all those 'old Africa hands' to whom we gave hospitality – veteran reporters, world-weary cameramen, former activists in an emerging Africa who could do a faultless Mugabe piece of mimicry or tell hilarious stories about a vast political bribe in Nigeria. Kit and Dick swapped many yarns about the enchanting, maddening continent.

What Dick liked about Kit was that he was essentially a Bohemian, which was the tribe with which my husband always identified. 'We're not middle class, we're not working class, we're not any of those categories – we're bohemians,' he'd say. Bohemians lived untidy lives, drank in Soho (drank anywhere, in fact), and were mainly interested in good conversation - not acquiring material things. (Dick was so eccentrically bohemian himself that he was against private washing machines: they were 'bourgeois', launderettes were acceptably collectivist.) Dick thought Kit was really one of us – at heart a true bohemian.

Thus I was taken aback when John Poppleton called Kit, in the TV documentary, an 'established pillar of the community.' True, Kit was occasionally wheeled on to TV programmes to comment upon some prominent person becoming a Catholic – the Duchess of Kent did so, for example. But I've been wheeled on to TV programmes myself to comment on some such event: all it means is that a TV researcher desperately needs a talking head and has happened upon the most available. Dick and I certainly didn't see Kit as a member of the Establishment. He was far too rackety. He was just like some rangey Fleet Street journo. (One of our friends that Kit liked best was Stan Gebler Davies – also now dead – who was an amiable, hopelessly disorganised, utterly anarchic shambles of a bulbous-faced journalist. His aunt, by marriage, was Edna O'Brien, who, eccentrically, he insisted on calling 'Aunt Josephine'. Kit and Stan travelled around Ireland together and had a hilarious, rumbustious, time.)

This friendship that Dick and I had with Kit Cunningham – which dated from the middle 1970s until the early years of the twenty-first century – was also a friendship of couples. From the 1970s onwards, Kit had a woman friend, Audrey Jones*, (who died, rather suddenly, from liver failure in 2007). Audrey was around my age: a fair-haired, handsome and capable woman with more than a passing resemblance to the young Margaret Thatcher. Audrey was commanding, kind-hearted, and could have an earthy sense of humour. Her grown-up children – she had been married and divorced - were offended when I wrote that no one could knew whether her relationship with Kit was sexual or not; they insisted that nothing improper had ever taken place between Audrey and Kit.

I did not mean to offend them, and they are in the best position to know. But if the relationship wasn't sexual, it was certainly loving. I travelled in Poland, Lithuania, Georgia and Russia with both Kit and Audrey, and I often shared a hotel room with Audrey Jones, as the ladies of the party were boarded out together. (I also travelled to Croatia with Audrey alone.) She confided to me how deeply she loved Kit and how she would do anything for him. I also saw Kit and Audrey covertly holding hands at the back of a coach rumbling across the Baltic states – hardly scandalous, but certainly indicating special attachment.

Audrey was also wholly involved in the parish and was accepted as the parish secretary, the de facto manager at St Etheldreda's, as well as Kit's constant companion. They never hid their friendship, and they behaved like a regular couple. I have a stack of holiday postcards signed "love from Kit and Audrey".

I certainly didn't disapprove of Audrey's friendship with Kit: how could I possibly be in a position to make such a judgement? But I did sometimes think it seemed indiscreet, considering he was the Rector of St Etheldreda's, and Catholic priests are supposed to be committed to manifest celibacy – a rule which I personally think is overdue for revision. Yet I did wonder if the Rosminian Order, or the relevant Bishop, might have issued a note of caution, and I subsequently discovered that a member of the church choir had contacted the Rosminian Provincial about the situation. Audrey was being nicknamed 'Mrs Cunningham' among some parishioners, and it was indeed giving rise to gossip. It was puzzling that the church authorities seemed to take no position on what was a very open couple relationship – even if it was celibate.

On one occasion, Kit asked me if he could borrow my one-bedroom rented flat in Dublin, so that he and Audrey could stay there. Crafty enough to envisage a headline in the *Irish Sun* newspaper – PRIEST IN LOVE-NEST IN CATHOLIC WRITER'S FLAT – I refused, offering a tactful excuse that my lease didn't permit me to lend the flat to friends.

Yet I didn't think he should have asked me for that favour, and I wondered, too, if I shouldn't say something about avoiding scandal – oh, yes, that weasel phrase. I also wondered why it was that no senior figure of clerical authority hadn't uttered a word of caution. Either you're against celibacy for the priesthood (which I am) or you're for it: whichever you favour, stand firm. There can be platonic friendships, to be sure; yet I knew the ways of the media, and however pure the friendship might have been, their constant and open togetherness might easily have popped up in Nigel Dempster's gossip column, or in *Private Eye*. At one stage, I even consulted Maeve Binchy – who was a sound source of agony-aunt advice and generally gave wise answers – asking her if I should say something about a priest being more discreet. Maeve advised me not to say anything. These were two adult people and it didn't do to meddle. Maeve and I had grown up in Dublin when there were far too many busybodies ready to report any priest seen with a woman not his sister to the ferocious Archbishop of Dublin, John Charles McQuaid. That kind of prying into people's relationships seemed odious. So, partly on Maeve's advice not to meddle, I left it.

But here's the irony of it: I was concerned that Kit might get into trouble for his friendship with a woman. And Audrey wasn't the only woman who was devoted to Kit either. There was a delightful woman, Rosemary Nibbs, who did secretarial work at St Etheldreda. She was utterly devoted to Kit and became a Catholic virtually on his account. (Previously, she had been a secretary to the late critic and writer Kenneth Tynan, to whom she also remained very loyal, despite some post-mortem revelations that weren't entirely edifying.) Kit was also dedicated to my friend Marjorie Wallace, and to her young daughter and he ran charitable fairs for SANE, Marjorie's mental health charity. Kit and Audrey would babysit Sophia when young, almost like foster-parents. And there were other personalities, particularly women, who were always ready to rally round Kit. He was exceptionally successful at bringing women into the Catholic church; Audrey was originally one of his converts.

After the scandal broke, some of these women remembered how kind Kit had been. My friend Sue Thomson, who is an Anglican and was not a parishioner, remembered how, after her mother died, Kit was the first to call around and really give her time and words of consolation. Lady Stubbs – the educationalist Marie Stubbs – spoke to me at length on the telephone about how supportive Kit had been in so many ways, and how much he had done for the common good. Alannah Hopkin, the Irish writer, emailed me from Kinsale in West Cork remembering how wonderfully helpful Kit had been to her after her first marriage broke down – Kit spoke so compassionately to her at a time when some Catholic priests were much less approachable for a divorced woman.

Another woman, Marie Strong, who had been on our travels to Eastern Europe – and whose parents, and subsequently her brother, Gaston Berlemont, had run the famous 'French House' in Soho, where so many of the Bohemian tribe drank – wrote to me to say how fondly she remembered Kit, how he went out of his way to help everyone on the tour and how responsibly he behaved when a problem arose for any of the group. When the late actor Michael Anthony, to whom Kit was very protective since he was an elderly widower, lost his tickets and passport and got confused on a nightmare coach journey from Vilnius to Warsaw, Kit was just so sweet and cheering to the old chap (we said prayers to St Anthony, and the documents turned up).

Michael Anthony's daughter, Frances Butlin, who remained friends with Kit after her father's death, simply couldn't bring herself to watch the TV documentary. She cherished the kindness that Kit had shown her father – actors, especially when old, can be vulnerable people – and she just couldn't face watching *Abused*. And even after the paedophile story was all over the papers, Frances stood by his memory to me: 'He was so incredibly kind and generous to my father, Michael and that made a great difference to him as he was growing older and in quite low water,' she said. 'Kit always invited him to Sunday lunch when Michael was in London – always encouraging to him and enabling him to travel with the companions of Ely Place. And when my father died, his support and guidance in arranging a beautiful funeral for Daddy was something to remember always.' She was devoted to Kit for being 'so inclusive of people and wanted them to enjoy Ely Place and everyone loved him for that. He persuaded people like my husband, Martin to come to church when they usually would not have even wanted to – and everyone enjoyed the experience at St Etheldreda's.'

Alenka Lawrence, another journalist friend now married and living in America, said that she was 'moved to tears' when reading about the paedophile scandal relating to Kit Cunningham. And yet, she added, 'despite everything I will always owe a lot to Fr Kit and his kindness. I remember when I took my fiancée to meet him at Ely Place, well before we were engaged, and Kit seemed to sense what was in the air and said to John with a conspiratorial wink – "Look after her – she's a sweetie!"" She was, of course, very upset about the revelations, but concluded that 'He was perhaps the type of flawed but eventually redeemed character that you find in Graham Greene – which is, after all, so very human.'

The same reaction occurred with so many of the people Kit had known. My friends Tony and Marisol Duff, who were married by Kit (on the day before Princess Diana died) at St Etheldreda's, were simply flabbergasted by the revelation that he stood accused of being a dangerous and predatory paedophile. Others were not only appalled, but rueful that they had thought so well of Kit. Peter Stanford articulated this in an article in the *Observer*. Peter had written a favourable obituary of Kit in the *Guardian*, and now he wrote that 'the sight of John Poppleton holding a copy of an obituary I wrote . . . for the *Guardian* made me feel profoundly ashamed.

'The subject was Father Kit Cunningham, the Catholic priest who had married us, baptised my son and was a family friend of twenty years. "A Technicolour eccentric, and widely loved as a consequence," the obituary read.' Mr Poppleton had dubbed this obit 'offensive . . . This priest was a monster.'

Peter wrote about his struggle to accept 'the sexual, physical and mental abuser', as Kit was described in an email to him, with the man he had known. He felt profoundly shaken because, 'I felt that Fr Kit was a priest I could trust'. Peter's article spoke for many.

I reacted perhaps more angrily, initially; I too was in denial. What I couldn't accept about the documentary was that words like 'monster' and 'ogre' could seem to sum up Kit's whole character. Is a man's life only his sins? The young people who had known Kit – my sons, my nephews, my niece, and many other young folk who had summer jobs in the City of London and knew Kit – had never had the slightest whiff of paedophile advances from him. There were no sexual advances, although women noticed that he could be flirtatious with them. One woman – one of his converts – went further and said he could be 'lecherous'. 'He needed watching – and a firm hand!'

So I found it difficult to put together the man I had known and the 'monster' portrayed by his accusers. Another writer, Jo Siedlecka, and I even spoke about writing a joint book to give the whole story of the man's life. We didn't get to follow this through, partly because both of us were too busy with other projects, and partly because I, anyway, lost heart. If it was true, that he had been described as a 'predatory paedophile', what was the point of trying to defend him? We know by now that we should put the victims first, rather than defend the perpetrator.

All the same, at another level, I felt I should be loyal to the memory of a friend, despite his sins, for the good things he had also done. There were historical parallels to evoke: Roger Casement was an egregious paedophile (perhaps, strictly speaking, a 'hebephile', since his fixation was on young boys on the cusp of adolescence), but he was still a brave and heroic man who revealed the horrors of slavery in the Belgian Congo and South America. Roger Casement's life is not assessed solely in the context of his obsession with young boys of eleven to thirteen: he is remembered as a patriotic Irishman (with an airport and a public park in Dublin called after him) and a brave voice against cruelty and slavery. And rightly so.

Yet, in our time, it seems that a paedophile offence is now the very worst sin a man can commit. I happened to be in Ireland when *Abused* was first broadcast. It was preceded, on the Northern Ireland network, by a programme about a former IRA woman who became a minister in the Belfast administration. Some people objected to the fact that this person, now in political office, had been convicted of murder during the Troubles. Others said 'that was then, and this is now' , and 'we are all now going forward with the peace process'. Had the lady been accused of paedophilia rather than murder, I don't believe she'd have had a cat's chance in hell of becoming a politician in office. I think we do regard a paedophile offence as being worse than homicide.

* * *

Later in 2011, I had a long conversation with the moral theologian Father Alexander Lucie-Smith, who had lived at St Etheldreda's for more than three years during Kit's tenure there. Alexander, who had also lived in Africa, was in no doubt whatsoever that the charges against Kit were true. He did abuse those young boys at Soni in Tanzania. And yet, Fr Lucie-Smith thought Kit was not essentially a paedophile. Sexuality will sometimes find an outlet which is not necessarily an inherent orientation. Sometimes sexuality defies complete analysis – we do not really know why people act the way they do.

For all the scores of accounts I have read about paedophile offenders, rare are the reports which seek to explain why a paedophile offends. It is almost an unexplored field in journalism-reportage.

And Fr Alex was right: Kit did have a bullying streak, he said, and in drink he could be aggressive and abrasive – which I conceded, and I had seen flashes of Kit's bad temper occasionally. Though I had more than enough experience of the ghastly things that people can do – including myself – in drink, and bad temper goes with that territory. It was the bullying side that emerged when Kit coerced those schoolboys to give him what is colloquially called 'hand jobs'. It was the abuse of power that was the wellspring of the offences. He did it because he could.

I think there was another context, too, and this was partly suggested to me in conversation with Fr David Myers, of the Rosminian Order who has had to take responsibility for this melancholy affair. Soni was a remote place: the school was lamentably badly run, some of the pupils there came from the notoriously decadent White Kenyans – the 'Happy Valley' set – and conceivably these children felt abandoned by their families in a lonely boarding school. Abuse, whether through the manipulation of power, through physical cruelty or through sexual acts, seldom takes place where children are protected by a caring family constellation. This may be an explanation, but it is not an excuse. Had the school been properly run, the situation could have been stopped, and corrected. It is a matter of exercising good authority, and good authority, in management, is essential.

And yes, individuals can have many facets to their characters, and a man may be a bully, and a drunk, too, yet also have a quite benign element to his character. That is why women take back abusive husbands again and again: because the violent bully can also be a charmer, and sweet, and a wonderful lover. People are complicated. One of Kit's accusers – not a direct victim, but one who was familiar with the situation – has repeatedly called him a 'psychopath'. I'd describe him as a sinner, but a psychopath is someone who has no feelings and cannot empathise, and none of the friends who had know Kit Cunningham over the past thirty years of his life in London would have described him thus.

* * *

Richard and I moved to Deal in Kent in 1997 and by the time the scandal broke, Richard was too frail to take it all in. He was inclined to suggest that English public schools were, in times gone by, dens of spanking, wanking and bullying anyway. He was sceptical about some of the claims – in the general culture – about sexual abuse. And by the turn of the twenty-first century, I had been seeing less of Kit and Audrey, partly because of distance, and also, because I had stopped drinking. When you quit drinking, boozy scenes become a bore, and drunks an almighty bore. Lunch at St Etheldreda's, which I'd once uproariously joined, now seemed something of an ordeal. There had been far too much drink taken during the high years of Kit's stewardship of St Etheldreda's.

I was, of course, sad when Audrey died, and puzzled by the suddenness of her death. She seemed reasonably well when I saw her in the November before her death, and then we had the news that she had gone to bed one night feeling off-colour, and experiencing some pain, and was discovered – by Kit, at St Etheldreda's, where she had stayed the night of her passing – to be lifeless the next morning. The reason for her death was given as liver failure, though it is surely unusual for this to occur suddenly. But I was told no more.

I knew Kit would be very lost after that. And he seemed weepy any time that I spoke to him, and his life began to deteriorate, one way and another. Those who he had abused began to contact him and confront him. He at first denied, and then conceded. Francis Lionnet, who spent hours over recent years talking to the Soni group, says it was down to cowardice. 'Two victims went to see [Kit] at St Etheldreda's. One . . . was over six feet tall, and on seeing the now fully grown man, Kit immediately fell to his knees and begged forgiveness. The other, a 5'7" guy whom he had frequently abused, turned up at St Eth's somewhat drunk in order to confront him. Kit ignored his questions and imperiously dismissed him.'

But it all caught up with him in the end, just the same. The story of Kit Cunningham is also a classic Greek tragedy: a man brought down, in the end, by his fatal flaw. Perhaps it was precisely because he knew he had committed serious wrongs against innocent young boys that Kit went out of his way to compensate, as it were, to make amends, by his many kindly deeds later in life. Perhaps he drank to blot out those memories – as they say in AA: 'I drank to drown my sorrows, but my sorrows learned to swim.' Perhaps, being a sinner himself, he was less judgemental of those who came to him with problems in their lives. But the Greek tragedy also unfolded in another sense too: all his life, he must have feared that this secret would come out, and indeed, as he moved towards the end of his life, it did.

I think pride also played a part in the downfall. Audrey was very anxious to obtain an honour for Kit, and she worked hard and lobbied widely for it. She sent me round-robins to sign and networked among the powers that be that he should be awarded an honour. And so, finally, an MBE was bestowed upon him. He had served St Etheldreda's, its music and congregation, and the community around it (including the hospitals where he also did chaplain duty), and MBEs are regularly awarded to people who perform services to the community in this way, so there was nothing amiss with his nomination.

He should never have accepted it. He should surely have 'called to mind his sins', and declined. Anything that puts a man, or a woman, in the spotlight, will shine a light also on the hidden corners of a life. Not that evading the spotlight diminishes the import of an offence: but a fall will be more public and more mortifying when the victims believe that the offender is preening and enjoying a successful lifestyle.

Because it was the knowledge and awareness of his MBE that particularly enraged former pupils at Soni, and got them linking up with each other on the web. Some have been in touch with me and said they were particularly furious that he should be garlanded with an honour (they also felt that he lived a life surrounded by dazzling celebrities, while their lives had been ruined by depression, thoughts of suicide and other psychological problems).

Audrey so cherished Kit that she pushed for his recognition by the Queen. And thus she unknowingly unleashed the signal for his downfall, which duly came, to the anguish and shame of his family and the bewilderment of his many friends. But the symmetry is exquisite: you shall reap as you sow.

I often wondered, when I read about a paedophile offence in the newspapers, what was the back story. And although the experiences of victims are often explored in the media, I have never yet read an account of why the offender did it: this is why I felt impelled to explore this more, and to try and understand it. But perhaps you never really come to understand the back story, or why people do what they do, except that human beings are not rational creatures, and often profoundly complex and disturbed. Of course I hope that all the victims from Soni find justice and, where possible, recompense for what they endured. First things first. But Kit's friends will still remember the good parts of his character with affection. As Frances Butlin says: 'Kit did everything *con amore*.'

There was an interesting coda to the BBC's strongly accusatory tone in Olenka Frenkiel's *Abused*. The following year it transpired that the BBC, as an institution, was less than vigilant in detecting child abuse among its own ranks, and even facilitated characters like Jimmy Savile to continue molesting and assaulting children over many decades – some of the victims as young as nine, and some were handicapped children. Subsequently the presenter Stuart Hall was sent to prison for his paedophile offences, which the BBC had again failed to investigate: the corporation certainly appeared in a complacent light.

By June of 2013, some 150 allegations of sexual abuse had been made against 81 employees of the BBC. The subject and terrain of *Abused* may be updated and revisited, but the slightly triumphalist air which broadcasters have brought to unveiling abuse among the clergy may possibly be nuanced by some sense of humility that terrible things happen elsewhere too: and *all* institutions that are not subject to checks and balances of a vigorous nature will be vulnerable to corruption. I think there was something in my penny Catechism about original sin which pointed to that: man's flawed nature, indeed.

Audrey Jones is a pseudonym: 'Audrey's' children do not wish her real name to be on the record. Audrey is the modern version of Etheldreda.

All Aboard the Condom Train
My side of the story

A couple of years ago the theatre director Lynne Parker – a director I much admire – wrote to me about a possible plan to turn the story of 'the condom train' into a musical, written by the witty and inventive Arthur Riordan (who did a brilliantly entertaining musical about John Betjeman and Ireland's neutrality). Would I cooperate in the research? I replied to Lynne that she and Arthur were welcome to any recollections that I had, although the event might be better suited to the genre of farce than to the musical.

I've had scores of MA and PhD students interview me over the years about the famous incident in May 1971 when the Irish Women's Liberation Movement (IWLM) carried off the theatrical stunt of purchasing condoms in Belfast, and bringing them to Dublin so as to deliberately break the 1935 law which prohibited 'birth control artefacts'.

At the last count, the event had appeared in ten books, including memoirs and novels. (Nell McCafferty got so fed up being asked about it she suggested we should charge a fee for any further interviews.) Kevin Myers has written that he thought it was the most ridiculous aspect of Irish historical perspectives that this minor episode was considered so significant. But that's the way of the world: a stunt which captures the imagination is often remembered better than an accurate and careful historical account of basic facts.

Most of the scholars who have researched the 'condom train' have first drawn on June Levine's book, *Sisters*, which I didn't altogether admire. I thought June's story was compelling when she wrote about herself and her own experiences as a frustrated wife in Canada; I didn't think June was a very objective reporter when it came to the bigger picture.

To be honest, June's report of the condom train irked me so much that for thirty years I couldn't read most of the book (and I developed a pedantic contempt for the description of my family's mid-Victorian home in Ballsbridge as 'Georgian': if she thinks 1853 is the same as 1753, I muttered to myself, it hardly speaks highly of her sense of history). Perhaps my pride was hurt when June wrote of me as an 'egomaniac'. Through all the years of our friendship, I always secretly resented what she had written about me in *Sisters*, and although I had much affection for June (and gratitude for her generosity – she was the most generous woman I ever knew), there was always a niggling reserve in my subconscious, and when she died I wondered if I had faked our friendship a little over-sedulously.

What she wrote became a source book for so many other studies, and even entered a reference book about Irish people, written by the left-wing *Irish Times* journalist Conor O'Cleary, in which I figure, exclusively, as someone who went about blowing up condoms like balloons. ('Bloody hell!' I exclaimed. 'I've worked my socks off as a journalist and writer for four decades and that's all that this guy can quote! A stupid and inaccurate statement from Levine – without even checking with me!')

So, before I die, I resolved to give my account of the the basic background and context to the 1971 event and this is it.

The importation of 'birth control devices' had been prohibited by the Irish State in 1935, and that prohibition had remained on the statute books for the following thirty-five years.

The Irish State was not alone in prohibiting contraception at that time – France had done likewise in 1920, and several American states also banned birth control. As the biographies of Margaret Sanger and Marie Stopes illuminate, in the early decades of the twentieth century, birth control was considered shocking and unacceptable (it was called 'race suicide', which might bring an ironic smile to the ageing, low-fertility populations of Europe, overtaken by the dynamic population surges in India and Brazil, or anywhere that Islam thrives). So Irish opposition to 'suppression of conception' was not unique. Agricultural societies, which regarded any form of barrenness as failure, were also more inclined to be hostile to the deliberate reduction of fertility than urban ones.

But by 1970 anti-birth control attitudes were becoming archaic in the wider world, and the Irish law needed to be abrogated. The contraceptive pill was legal and did not come under the prohibition, as it was not a 'device' but a medication*, but all barrier methods and spermicides – which were favoured by those who used birth control in the 1930s – did. Marie Stopes was an especial advocate of the 'Dutch cap' – the rubber diaphragm that women self-inserted.

It would take a decade and more to change this 1935 law completely, and the men and women in Dail Eireann were not particularly keen to embarrass themselves by addressing the situation. Indeed, my recollection is that, in 1970, only one TD, the late Dr John O'Connell – an inner-city GP who had experience of women's health issues – was outspokenly supportive, within the political realm, of contraceptive freedom. Not even vaunted liberals like Conor Cruise O'Brien had anything to say on the matter in the public realm. (To be fair, Irishmen in the past often felt it was 'indecorous' to breach these matters openly, rather as parents dread having a sex education talk with their children.) And so, we in the IWLM, decided to move for change with this initiative of 'the condom train'. (It is sometimes called 'the contraceptive train', which is factually wrong, as not all contraceptives fell under the prohibition. And even seasoned birth controllers say that celibacy, abstinence and gay sexual relationships are also forms of 'contraception' – if you want to be clear about the many ways of not conceiving. The 'rhythm method' of observing the natural fertility cycles of women was considered laughable – too uncertain, and expecting men to exercise self-control – although it has since had a revival in the study of fertility.)

I don't remember exactly who thought up the condom train stunt: it may have been me, it may have been a collective decision that emerged at one of our IWLM meetings, which sometimes took place in my flat in Dublin 4, and had originally begun at Margaret Gaj's restaurant in Baggot Street. The genesis of the IWLM is conscientiously, if a little earnestly, told by an American academic, Anne Stopper, in her book *Mondays at Gaj's: The Story of the Irish Women's Liberation Movement*. Ms Stopper is correct in saying that contraception was identified by those of us working in journalism as a choice, a freedom and an entitlement that was denied to Irishwomen. It was also an area of women's health that needed attention. Safe reproductive health should always be a priority in any political system.

There were other reforms and changes required, too, including the 'marriage bar', which meant that married women could not be employed by the state, or a number of other statutory bodies; financial autonomy (women couldn't open a bank or store account without the counter-signature of a man); and the right to be called to jury service (which women had had at the foundation of the Irish state in 1923, but which they had lost in 1927, partly because women so often cried-off jury service that the Free State administration concluded it was easier to excuse females altogether.) But contraception was, in every sense of the word, the 'sexiest' of these themes of female emancipation and made for deliciously provocative banner-headlines.

A stunt is often a good way to move political ideas forward: the Suffragettes had done it with their demonstrations – some of which were hair-raisingly violent, and environmental organisations like Friends of the Earth and Greenpeace have been imaginative in their various forms of direct action. So a trainful of us feminists travelled to Belfast for the day to equip ourselves with the contraceptive devices, returning to Dublin brandishing them at the customs at Connolly Station. (The hated border that girdled the six counties, keeping it 'British' and separating it from the Irish Republic, turned out to be handy after all.)

And that is what we did, we radical feminists on the condom train. Among many others there was Nell McCafferty, Marin Johnston, June Levine, Monica McEnroy, Marie McMahon, Mary Anderson, Caroline de Costa, Bernadette Quinn, Colette O'Neill, Mary Sheerin, and myself – altogether a high-spirited and intelligent group of women for whom I had, and retain, great regard.

There were absentees: Mary Maher of the *Irish Times*, a prominent feminist, was having a baby (and was not entirely sure that the stunt wouldn't look frivolous). Mairin de Burca, a strongly politicised activist, chose not to join: as a single woman committed to celibacy, she felt it wasn't her place to claim contraception, a decision that was characteristic of Mairin's honesty.

Nuala Fennell, who was to become our first Minister for Women, also chose not to join the exercise. Nuala was concerned that the lack of dignity necessarily involved could actually harm our image. The poet Eavan Boland, who often attended our meetings, also declined to get embroiled in such a spectacle.

Mary Robinson, who was simultaneously pursuing the case for contraceptive rights through the constitutional route, also disdained to be one of the band: she was to become our first female president of Ireland, but Mary had led an academic's ivory-tower life and was never one to get down and dirty with agitprop. You couldn't imagine her purchasing condoms in some Belfast pharmacy. Had she required such items, you feel she'd have sent her maid. Mary, however, was stalwart and dogged in changing the law through the courts and the constitution (she was a great admirer of Daniel O'Connell for pioneering change through the law.) Another feminist, Rosita Sweetman, spent the day in bed with her lover, which seemed a more poetic illumination of what it was all about.

And so the group went about their task of obtaining the Belfast contraceptives (mostly condoms and spermicides – this was pretty much all you could get over the counter. Other 'devices', such as the diaphragm or the coil had to be properly fitted by a family planning doctor or nurse.)

What I now remember most vividly about this event was what I felt. I knew that this was something which had to be done, because it would make a point dramatically, sensationally, even historically. But I was also wretched about doing it. I knew how upset my mother would be – how mortified to see her daughter in the headlines, even identified as a ringleader, in a stunt which involved buying French letters in Belfast. 'Refinement' and 'decorum', along with 'respectability' had been values so ardently pursued by Irishwomen of my mother's, and grandmother's, generation – values which distanced them from the squalor, drudgery and coarseness of much of rural life. I hated throwing all that back in her face.

Once in Belfast, I separated from the others and did what I often do when I want to escape from reality, to forget the corner into which I have painted myself: I went to the movies. It was an Ursula Andress-Stanley Baker romantic comedy, *Perfect Friday*, and I could subsume my anxieties for the afternoon in the half-empty cinema.

But the real-life programme proceeded, and I rejoined the group at the Belfast train station, equipped with whatever it was I needed to have. And so the train departed for Dublin once again and many of the women on board were in happy-go-lucky form. We were joined by ordinary shoppers, but word spread that this larky feminist group were about to pull something dramatic.

In June Levine's account (on which Anne Stopper draws), I was described as behaving disgracefully on the journey back to Dublin. I was 'beside myself with excitement', June wrote. She claimed that I greatly offended a woman sitting with a child in the train, that my conversation was so scandalous that the woman departed from the carriage to protect the child from my revolting conversation. I have no recollection of this episode. I admit that I could be outrageously shocking in my conduct, although that was usually under the influence of alcohol, and in a mood of high exuberance. My mood that day was far from exuberant. It was low and brooding, and I didn't have a drink until much later in the evening.

At Connolly Station in Dublin, the birth control 'artefacts' were duly declared, and the demonstration was manifestly an immediate success: the customs men were pink in the face with embarrassment (or slyly tickled behind it all) and declined to take any action, such as a public confiscation of the contraband, or arresting those in possession of same. The law had been challenged, and successfully breached. There was an atmosphere of carnival at the Dublin railway station – formerly called Amiens Street – and some of the activists began blowing up condoms like balloons. June Levine claims that I was the main agent of this infantile endeavour, while she, self-portrayed as the reliable one, was obliged to 'restrain' me.

It is my contention that what June Levine wrote about me was a fantasy. It was the Marie-Antoinette syndrome: legend has ascribed to Queen Marie-Antoinette that she said of the starving peasantry: 'Let them eat cake'. The lady said no such thing (naively, she did once ask: 'Why do they have no brioche?') but 'let them eat cake' has always been ascribed to her because it *seems to fit her character*.

June thought of me as the kind of madcap, reckless, harum-scarum, daredevil – manipulative and egomaniacal, too – who, typically, *would* inflate condoms like balloons; and so she ascribed that action to me. She saw what she wanted to see. My own recollection is completely different. When we arrived at Connolly Station, I felt so subdued by the whole undertaking that I hung back in the train, dawdling and dreading the barrage of cameras and lights that would meet us at the exit. This is why there is no footage of me, and no media photographs of me, associated with the condom train. I also deplored the schoolgirlish squealing that went on at the top of the line. I remember thinking 'why do women's voices in a group sound so shrill?' By the time I alighted from the train, trailing behind the other passengers, the action was over.

Later on that evening, I did go on RTÉ's *Late Late Show*, with Colette O'Neill, and spoke about the episode and how we had travelled to Northern Ireland deliberately to break an archaic law. (RTÉ wiped the tape – they wiped all the tapes of the first twenty-five years of the *Late Late Show*. As, earlier, they had wiped the audio voice of W. B. Yeats – unlike the BBC, which conserved everything.)

Yes, on the night in question I held up the condoms for the TV camera (discreetly wrapped in their packets, and not inflated) to make the point that the law had been successfully challenged, and no one arrested. And this leads to another aspect in the saga of the Irish Women's Liberation Movement.

As both June Levine and Anne Stopper have written, my reputation was regarded with a mixture of awe and suspicion: how brilliant I was at attracting publicity, and drawing attention to myself, as well as to the cause! June, and some others, regarded me as an arrant self-publicist and they were exasperated that once again I was hogging the limelight by appearing on national television as an apparent self-appointed leader of women's liberation. The truth was that I appeared on the *Late Late Show* because Pan Collins, the studio power behind the host, Gay Byrne, decided that I should represent one aspect of the sisterhood, and Colette O'Neill, who was then a housewife, should represent another. I didn't put myself forward: I was asked to do the gig. I was uncomfortable about doing it, but you have to take responsibility for your actions and follow things through. But it wouldn't have been my choice.

The condom train was a successful stunt because it did help to lead, eventually, to an outdated law being rescinded, through the proper legislative channels. It happened too slowly for some – condoms and other birth control devices were at first only made available for married couples, but then birth control had proceeded in most other societies in a gradualist way, too. Until the 1970s, women in Britain seeking the Pill had to be married (or pretend to be) or engaged (or pretend to be). I remember very well friends in London passing around a fictitious 'engagement ring', which they wore when attending a family-planning clinic.

After the condom train episode, I avoided meeting my mother for quite some time, as I knew I would have hurt her – that was the brooding feeling that had hovered over me all the way from Belfast. Interestingly, when I got to speak to her some years later about the general subject of family planning, it transpired that she wasn't against the Pill; I think this was because the Pill was discreet, and clinical, and removed from the actual act of sexual intercourse. (Ironically, if the Pill had been around when she was in her childbearing years – as she indicated at another point in conversation – I would probably never have been conceived!)

But Ma couldn't talk about condoms. They were, in her time, strongly associated with the prevention of disease from prostitutes – soldiers in the First World War were issued with them when attending French brothels. As it happens, with the appearance of AIDS, condoms once again came to be seen as prophylactics against sexually transmitted disease. On a personal note, I might add, I have never liked the condom. Placing a piece of vulcanised rubber between lovers' skin-to-skin contact strikes me as about as erotic as swimming in a woollen onesie. It also places all the power of birth control with the man, and may thus remove a woman's choice. For some women, the condom is a source of 'male withholding'. But that does not alter the fact that this is not an area where the heavy hand of the state should intervene: the state should stay out of citizens' bedrooms, unless assault, rape or threats to life are involved.

Our sensational demonstration became a footnote in social history, and a source of continued notoriety that would last all our lives. If I had my time over again, I think I would rather have chosen the Mary Robinson route, and challenge the law through the courts and the Irish Constitution, which affirms personal and family rights, and was used creatively and dexterously by Mary, as a lawyer. That surely was the dignified and sensible way. But the dignified and sensible way was not, in my twenties, my natural reflex, which rather sought excitement, sensation and general high jinks.

*The contraceptive pill was legally available in the Republic of Ireland: I, and others I knew, had no difficulty obtaining a prescription for it. Some doctors declined to prescribe it and some doctors preferred to call it a 'cycle regulator'. But the objective fact was that it was labelled and presented in exactly the same package as in the United Kingdom, bearing the pharmaceutical description 'anovulent'. If some doctors, and their patients, chose to call it fairy dust, that didn't change the pharmacological facts.)

Sexual Liberation
Dottie Parker was my role model

They had a somewhat restricted view, in Sandymount, Dublin 4, of what was suitable reading for a schoolgirl in the late 1950s; my uncle had confiscated an Agatha Christie mystery from me, pronouncing the subject of murder to be 'squalid' and 'disedifying' for the tender consciences of a young lady. Actually, I had come upon reading matter that was much more subversive and this other book signalled to me, soul to soul.

It was a slim volume of verse called *Enough Rope*, written by Dorothy Parker (first written in 1926, reprinted many times), acquired by my elder sister. As soon as I opened the pages, I felt that I entered Dottie Parker's world of New York speakeasies, cocktails, cigarette holders, daring, doomed love affairs, and sassy, wisecracking Manhattan gals who could take care of themselves.

This was sophistication! The details of Dorothy Parker's life I only learned later, but all the counter-cultural messages seemed to be hidden in the sub-text and I picked up, intuitively, on all that Mrs Parker (she was always called either Mrs Parker, or Dottie) was expressing.

Reading those sardonic verses about suicide attempts ('Razors pain you/Rivers are damp . . .') and the faithless men who break your heart in two – as opposed to those who never look at you – I somehow knew that Dorothy Parker was just like me. I just knew she'd been a troublesome pupil at her convent school – later expelled – and I knew that she had launched forth independently into a free and bohemian life just as I planned to do. And I knew she didn't give a damn for convention or for all those virtuous people who always got the glittering prizes in this life – or the next: those who love too much, she wrote, would go to hell with Helen of Troy – while 'those whose love is thin and wise/May view John Knox in paradise.'

As for men not making passes at girls who wear glasses – what a hoot! Surely a sally against those prim studious types always appointed the class prefect.

I just knew that Dorothy Parker drank too much – much too much; and long before I read her witticisms that 'one more drink and I'll be under the host', I aspired to being a Dorothy Parker acolyte. I was delighted to learn that she especially enjoyed boozing during the Prohibition era because it was against the law. She was perfection.

It endorsed all my intuitions to know that Dottie hated domesticity and her kitchen fridge was empty save for a bottle of Martini and some ice cubes. It was all there in the allusions of her poetry. You could see she was the antidote to the good housewife, and the polar opposite of the virtuous women we were expected to emulate – from Joan of Arc to Elizabeth Fry, of whom one might well approve, but bad girls need role-models too.

Yet in Dorothy Parker's verse the rebellion was beguilingly mixed with vulnerability, with ruefulness and yearning. ('Joy stayed with me a night – Young and free and fair – And in the morning light/He left me there.') Unlike the later liberated New Yorkers of *Sex and the City*, she is lyrical about failure and mistakes and the price of freedom.

Later in my teens I went on to read more of her poetry and her short stories, which were brilliant vignettes of life observed. These often described the lonesomeness of women when love goes astray. Although they can sometimes be satirical, they are less humorous than much of the poetry, and occasionally political. I remember being captivated by 'Soldiers of the Republic', a memorable account about the gallantry of poor men she encountered during the Spanish Civil War (she considered herself communist, but never voted in her life). She wrote a poignant short story about a woman being visited in hospital after an abortion – drawn on her own raw experience – which is remarkable accomplishment: not once is the word abortion mentioned, but you know exactly what is going on.

Only subsequently, too, did I read about the Algonquin table where her gang outdid one another in bitchy repartee: Dottie's pithy and caustic line about the actress who 'ran the gamut of emotions from A to B', and her sharp tongue about the society girls at Yale ('If all these sweet young things were laid end to end, I wouldn't be at all surprised'). She could be self-deprecating ('I was the toast of two continents – Greenland and Australia') and disparaging of her lovers, always handsome men ('his body went to his head'). She surely spoke for all writers when she said that the two most beautiful words in the English language were 'cheque' and 'enclosed'.

She was mixed-up and flawed – isn't everyone? She was intolerant of bores and though Jewish on her father's side – born Dorothy Rothschild, although no relation to the banking family – she could make anti-semitic cracks, though maybe that was a kind of Woody Allen-ism *avant la lettre*. She was self-destructive and one of her biographers considered her a despairing person. Her life was in many ways tragic.

She didn't age well and became to some degree reclusive (though I love what she said about the telephone ringing: 'What fresh hell is this?') She died more or less alone – though there were friends – and more or less without money – though there were uncashed cheques all around her disordered apartment – but she gallantly left her estate to Martin Luther King for the National Association for the Advancement of Colored People. She had no children – after that regretted abortion, she did conceive a much-wanted baby with her second husband, but to her bitter disappointment there was a miscarriage. Both her husbands died in circumstances that suggested suicidal intent, though possibly through mishap.

Her poetry was wonderfully defiant and witty, but the implication of pain was all there, and teenagers identify with tragedy: everyone has their *Young Werther*. Books read in youth often make an impact on an awakening mind, but there are not many I could return to now, without a veteran's critical reflexes or a sense that their themes have been overtaken by time. Yet I still possess that well-worn little volume of *Enough Rope*, and it still brings an evocative response. I remember how it took me out of Sandymount, Dublin 4, when I was fifteen; how it made me dream, aspire, dare and fantasise.

Part Five
On A Personal Note . . .

Dublin 4 Made Me

When I was a young child we lived in one of those big, old Victorian houses in Ballsbridge, Dublin. The house was called 'Gainsboro', but all the family called our home 'Herbert Road', because that is where it was located. Herbert Road's most famous claim to fame, at the time, was that it was virtually a continuation of Lansdowne Road, where all the great international rugby games were played, now called the Aviva Stadium. So a rugby football field that had been called after a Kerryman, Lord Lansdowne – he was a fierce Unionist and led the Irish peers in the House of Lords against Home Rule, but he was a Kerryman just the same – now bears the name of a British multinational corporation. Perhaps that's a metaphor of changing sources of power and influence in Ireland from the 1900s to the 2000s.

Anyway, there we were living in Herbert Road, which was a nice old house, if somewhat ramshackle – in winter you had to sleep under six blankets because of the cold; my parents could never really afford to do all the maintenance that an old house needs. And one afternoon, my aunty Dorothy and uncle Jim came to tea, and the conversation went something like this:

Aunty Dorothy, to my mother, Ita: 'You're so fortunate, Ita, to have had four children. We were very disappointed not to have had a family. Very disappointed.'

My mother, who must have been feeling more than usually fatigued and worried that day, replied 'Take one of mine! Take Mary! Please!'

Ita had been widowed two years previously and was having a hard time managing things. I was seven years old, and completely and totally wild. Nobody could control me. I did as I pleased, but what I pleased wasn't always pleasant. Sometimes it was very bold indeed.

One day Ita and I were walking by the River Dodder, near our house, when I espied a man fishing with a fishing-line in the river: next to him, standing on the wall, was his little dog, who was barking vociferously, as dogs do. For no particular reason, it came into my head to push the dog into the river, so I placed my childish hand on the terrier's bottom and – push! – plunged him into the Dodder River.

There was, apparently, the most terrible scene. The dog's owner nearly had apoplexy. He thundered and grew red in the face, denouncing my mother for the utterly evil child she had brought into the world.

I smirked away, pleased with myself for creating such a scene. I imagine the dog swam to the river bank – dogs can swim, can't they?

I also ran away from home constantly, from the age of about five. Not because I was unhappy – so far as I know – but because I just liked the freedom of it. I had a great passion for cars, and would constantly climb into the motor cars of strange men. Sometimes I would ask them to bring me 'for a spin' and buy me sweets. Is it a sign of the safety of the 1950s that never, ever did I come to any harm on these adventures? Strange men brought me for a drive and bought me sweets, and delivered me home safely.

But poor Mother. Small wonder she felt she couldn't control me. Aunty Dorothy, who, as it happens, had much practice in training dogs, thought herself more equal to the task.

I was delighted with myself about this new development, and the general fuss that was being made over me in the plan, which duly took hold, that I would move from my mother's home in Herbert Road, to the home of my uncle and aunt, just two streets away, in Oaklands Drive. It wasn't considered an unusual family arrangement, and no social services were involved. Wasn't fosterage an ancient Irish practice anyway? And maybe more than Irish. In *Mansfield Park*, Jane Austen's heroine, Fanny, is despatched off to live with a wealthier uncle and aunt.

* * *

'Dublin 4', in the 1950s, didn't have the same meaning as it has today, where it tends to signal affluence, high house prices, and a kind of metropolitan elitism which is thought to disdain grassroots Irish values. Dublin 4 wasn't – in my recollection – especially posh when I was growing up. The posh part of Dublin was Rathgar – illustrated by the grand lady who wanders into Seán O'Casey's play *The Plough and the Stars* 'from Rathmines'. Dublin 4 had a very grand part – where the embassies were, around Ailesbury Road, Shrewsbury Road and Merrion Road. But Donnybrook had had a reputation for being rough. Ballsbridge was *respectable*, and had always had more than a fair sprinkling of 'Southern Unionists' – the olden-days Protestants (and some Catholics) who still felt an attachment to the Crown.

The Royal Processions of Victoria, Edward VII and George V – with their carriages, heralds in tabards, and Royal Irish Lancers – had always halted at Ballsbridge on their journey from Dun Laoghaire (Kingstown) to Dublin Castle. But Ballsbridge also had corporation cottages and modest terraced homes – modest, but very attached, indeed, to respectability, which was the prevailing aspiration of the time.

There wasn't much of a centre to Ballsbridge: nowhere, really, where residents might stop and gossip. It had a row of shops and three famous institutions, the Royal Dublin Society, which hosted the Dublin Horse Show and had a fine library (there was also a decent public library), the Irish Bloodstock Sales ground – now gone replaced by Allied Irish Banks, this being another metaphor of the switch from horse and cattle trade to the dominion of bankers, and the Swastika Laundry, by the Dodder River.

Overseas visitors, especially from England, were somewhat taken aback to see the Swastika vans from the Swastika laundry ferrying cleaning around Dublin. When it was suggested to the owner of this old-established institution, in the 1940s, that he might, er, change his symbol – considering it was by then everywhere associated with the Nazi rule of the Third Reich – he was said to have replied: 'But I had the Swastika first!' Indeed, the swastika is a very old Indo-European logo, but there are some things that are too big to challenge, and the Nazis surely copyrighted the swastika. In time, Ballsbridge's Swastika laundry did indeed disappear.

We lived between Ballsbridge and Sandymount. Sandymount was a village by the sea and it had more character. It had shops, a post office, a village green, the wonderful Monument Creameries, two leading groceries, Findlaters and Leverett & Frye's (meticulously clean Protestant shops where you paid by despatching a little box travelling across a hanging wire) pharmacies, hairdressers, and three Churches: Methodists, in the village itself, Presbyterian and Catholic, further up along the road towards the city. (Further still, about a quarter of a mile towards Dublin city, at Irishtown, was the Church of Ireland, St Matthews, which is a pretty eighteenth-century ediface, and where the last mournful strains of 'God Save the King' were heard among the congregation just before Ireland left the Commonwealth in 1949.)

The Catholic Church ('the Star of the Sea') had three priests, none of whom, as far as I can recall, interfered with our lives in any noticeable way. (My parents, anyway, had their own Jesuit friends, who would visit us for afternoon tea – silver service brought out – and talk about Balzac.) The Sandymount priests seemed rather shy: one of them, Father Gunning, had albino-white eyelashes, and was painfully bashful, but he could deliver a Mass in fifteen minutes flat, which made his Masses remarkably popular. One of the trio, Father O'Connell, looked like the film star Tyrone Power and was, by all accounts, a fine hand at Bridge, and thus very popular with the Sandymount ladies – invited out every night of the week, by all accounts.

It was thought natural that women had more affinity with priests (since they were the priests' mothers, anyhow). Men might, of course, be very religious, but young men often stood outside the church doors during the sermon, going for a smoke. They also thought it was funny to trip up over-devout folks going up to Holy Communion (according to my brothers). There was a disparaging name for the over-devout: 'craw-thumpers'. You didn't want to be seen to be a craw-thumper.

One day a neighbour told my mother how she had gone to Confession to one of the Sandymount priests to explain that she was about to marry a Protestant. 'And why don't you marry a Catholic?' asked he (possibly Father Gunning, as I have a notion he was from the North). 'A Catholic never asked me,' said she. 'Fair play to you then – as long as he's a good man.' And that Protestant husband was a very good man indeed.

The local general pratictioner, Dr Young, was known to be an atheist. This was respected, but pitied. Sure, something terrible must have happened to him, to turn him bitter. It was said that an order of nuns in Gibraltar had refused succour to a dying patient of his, for fear of infection, and after that he would have nothing to do with the clergy. He was unmarried – or, possibly, a widower – and 'took a drink', which was the euphemism for a serious alcohol problem. People thought he seemed lonely, as he sat alone in his house at the top of Newbridge Avenue, one light bulb on. But he was regarded as a skilled and dedicated doctor, and 'call Dr Young' was a signal that a caring physician would soon be in attendance.

Sandymount, unlike Ballsbridge, was full of people who stopped in the street to gossip. It's something you see in a Caneletto painting, and is a sign of a community, even where malice – or 'backbiting', as it was known – laces the chatter. Sandymount also had a more literary history: James Joyce set a chapter of Ulysses on Sandymount Strand, and William Butler Yeats lived on the seafront at Sandymount for many years.

In moving those two streets from Herbert Road to Oaklands Drive, I moved marginally nearer to Sandymount. But in another way, I moved between two different worlds.

* * *

My parents' home, Gainsboro, was so easy-going that Lizzie Slevin – an alarmingly forthright woman from Ringsend who had acted as a kind of mother's help when my parents could afford it – called it 'Liberty Hall'. I never saw a key to our house: the side door was open permanently, and you just lifted the latch and walked in. And all kinds of people did just that. There were always people in that house – family, friends, cousins, lodgers, people who just invited themselves for the day, or for a few days. A friend of my mother's, Maud, came to lunch every Sunday, whether invited or not. It was accepted that if Maud needed lunch, she should have it. Maud was a qualified doctor but wouldn't practise medicine to spite her husband, whom she disliked: 'let him support me', she snapped. I couldn't understand this, as a child. If you were entitled to be a doctor, why wouldn't you be one?

There was an American young woman who stayed with us for about six months, and nobody quite knew who she was or why she was there. But she turned up on the doorstep, apparently on the recommendation of some Boston cousin, and just stayed. She had no money, and my brother James purchased her clothes for her from his modest salary as a young bank clerk. Eventually, some friend or relation of the family, who considered that this was taking Christian charity too far, managed to move her on. We never really did discover who she was or why she was in Ireland. Perhaps it was an unhappy love affair.

An elderly cousin of my mother's, Onnie Mulkerrin, came to live with us as a paying guest in the early 1950s. Onnie had been 'out' in 1916, and had a religious devotion to Mr de Valera. She wore handwoven tweeds and Irish-made clothes, as had been the vogue in the 1916 period. She was a retired schoolteacher, who had lived many years in England, and she took it upon herself to teach me to read. I was a child of quite spectacular restlessness – I am quite sure, now that I was afflicted by Attention Deficit Hyperactivity Disorder – and that took patience, on Onnie's part, to keep me quiet enough to follow the words on the page. But I remember the moment when they began to make sense. And I remember Cousin Onnie saying, 'concentrate, Mary: you can do more than you think you can, if you just persevere.' I sometimes call to mind those words today, in my own old age.

As well as Sunday lunch, there was always an evening meal around half-past six or seven o'clock, at Gainsboro. This was often a lively affair with much conversation and it might take a couple of hours. I was wild by nature, and I was allowed to run wild, probably because no one could control me. I cycled across Dublin when I was five, from Herbert Road to Ballymun. I ran across parapets which linked the high front door with the garage. My brothers and my sister were much older than me, so they were often either away at school or away somewhere else – Paris, most likely. There was a tradition of going to Paris. When in doubt, go to Paris. My mother really was quite poor, as a widow, but I got the feeling that while there wasn't always enough money to pay the electricity bill, money could always be found to go to Paris. In my heart, I still think this a sound principle, though I know Aunty Dorothy didn't approve of it. 'If you can't afford it,' she would say, 'go without!'

Although my father died when I was five (he had been sixty-seven when I was born) his memory was transmitted and preserved with great tenderness, and his values lived on. My parents regarded themselves as artistic people – that category known, in the French Communist Party, as 'bourgeois Bohemians'. Their critics, if they had any, would have called them airy-fairy. My aunty Dorothy, who was a critic, although she kept it reasonably well under wraps, considered my Ma as being 'airy-fairy'. Head in the clouds! Tastes above their pocket and ideas above their station. Ma and Da thought it vulgar to talk about money. Which was probably why they never had any.

Ma liked to drink China tea – lapsong souchong – with her pals (if possible at the Shelbourne or Gresham hotel). Aunty Dorothy simply thought this an 'affectation'.

Gainsboro had an absent-minded magic: there were rooms full of books – many in French and Spanish – and jumbles of pictures and fine china, which Ma adored. But when I moved to Oaklands Drive, I moved to the ordered universe of suburbia.

* * *

The houses in Oaklands Drive had been built in the 1940s in what had become the classic suburban style of the familiar kind – reception room, dining room, kitchen, and upstairs three bedrooms and a bathroom. Aunty Dorothy was a very ordered housekeeper: everything was done according to her weekly programme: Monday washday, Tuesday ironing-day, Wednesday do the silver, Thursday brush down the stairs, Friday go to the hairdresser. She would never, ever do her laundry on a Sunday, but that wasn't just because of her sense of order, it was also because Dorothy came from a Protestant – and as she was often pleased to say, a Cromwellian – background in County Tipperary. The family had brought the children up as Catholics, in an unusual case of land conversion: the relation that left them a fine farm of land in the beautiful Golden Vale had stipulated that they turn Papist.

Convert for 200 acres of Tipperary land? No contest! But although Aunty Dorothy was nominally Catholic – indeed, she was always dutiful about carrying out her religious duties – her culture was Protestant. I say this with no sectarian intent, for, in Sandymount, we grew up playing with Protestant children, and we were all on harmonious neighbourly terms.

169

The Catholic children envied the Protestants because they didn't have to go to Confession on a Saturday; and the Protestant children envied the Catholics because we were allowed to go to the pictures on a Sunday. And that was one of Aunty Dorothy's Protestant elements: she retained a certain view of what you could, and could not do, on a Sunday. Doing your laundry was one of them. She was almost, but not quite, reconciled to playing cards on Sunday. That is, she might do it, but seldom without a reflection on its forbidden character.

So here I was transported from my own family home – 'Liberty Hall' – to a much more correct and suburban setting, where there was a set of rules and regulations laid down, not cruelly, but with a regular discipline. Evening tea-time was on the dot of 6 o'clock, and if a guest were late, they missed their meal: nothing interfered with the habit of sitting down to a meal at exactly 6 o'clock. Bed-times were set at an exact time, too. At seven years of age, I had to be tucked up by 7.30 PM. Then it was 8 PM. Eventually it was 9 PM. But no lassitude was given. At Liberty Hall I could go to bed whenever I pleased.

Aunty Dorothy and Uncle Jim gave me what a child needs to have: the total focus on her best interest, though I didn't appreciate such novelties as being taken to the dentist. I had my own room and I was allowed to choose the wallpaper and the pictures to hang on the wall. The order and regularity were almost certainly beneficial, although the bedtime rules also developed in me a sneaky and deceptive streak, and I would secretly read, either by torchlight or by straining to see by the landing light. That is always the problem with rules and regulations: they promote order but they may entice duplicity.

* * *

I think everyone's childhood is interesting, and, as a journalist, whenever I've had the assignment of doing an interview, I always ask about a person's childhood. Childhood shapes the character. The Jesuit saying: 'Give me the child until he is seven, and I will give you the man' – originally about the beneficial effect of a sound early formation – has so much truth in it. But it's not the whole truth. We now know that genes play a significant part in the forming of personality.

I am especially interested in the nature versus nurture debate because, while I am physically, and in personality, very like my mother – I look at pictures of myself now and think, 'I have become my mother' – I also had a different influence, of this second, foster-mother, from the age of seven. And although I am definitely my mother's daughter, the influence of my aunt and uncle also proved quite enduring.

I have inherited much, in character, as well as in physical form from my mother, especially all those aspirations to be arty and cultured. And then from my aunt, that sense of Protestant duty. The desire to run away to Paris battles with the restraints of what must be done, for reasons of moral obligation.

Aunty Dorothy used to say, if you said you had a cold on a Sunday morning and cried off going to Mass, but then rallied impressively by the afternoon: 'If you're not well enough to go to church, you're not well enough to go to the pictures.' Duty before pleasure. And I still say that to myself. 'Get the work done, Mary, before you have the treat.' I'm not neat and tidy, and I'm a dreadful clutterbug – as my mother was – but I am ordered in the sense that I live each day according to a list of tasks which must be done: and despite a rackety, and heavy-drinking life in youth, I don't think I have ever missed a newspaper deadline.

Ireland in the 1950s is usually portrayed as an authoritarian and repressive place, and of course it was, in many ways – that's why we rebelled against it in the 1960s – but in other ways, especially at Gainsboro, life was easy-going and even, yes, I would use the word liberal.

My mother was liberal, for example, on attitudes to homosexuality – mainly because of her life-long love for Oscar Wilde. When she was a schoolgirl with the Ursuline nuns in Sligo in about 1920, she was dared by her fellow-classmates to ask a nun: 'Why was Oscar Wilde sent to jail?' The reason for Wilde's incarceration wasn't openly spoken about at this time (although there was always an Irish rumour that he was imprisoned for Fenian activities). The nun was an enlightened teacher called Mother Scholastica. She turned around from the blackboard and said quite coolly:

'Oh, just for loving another man.' And that was that. Ma couldn't see any problem with it. Although I think she would have considered it 'unromantic' for any couple, or individual, to be too explicit about intimate conduct.

My parents really did hold, for the most part, an attitude of Christian charity towards all. One of my mother's favourite sayings was: 'It would be a poor world if we were all the same.' That is a motto for tolerance and diversity. A few houses away from us on Herbert Road lived a colourful spinster named Mary Gaynor. She made – and wore – eccentric hats (though she made them very well) and collected paintings, and painters. Out of the blue she announced one day that she had lost her virginity at the age of forty-four. This was regarded as amusing because of the way she said it. She had found a painter whose work Mary purchased and displayed, and even persuaded Ma to purchase one of this lover's art works, which really was a meaningless daub, in the style of Rothko, but without the beguilement. Mary spoke in terms of wild exaggeration – 'Ghastly!' 'Extraordinary!' 'Beyond peradventure!' – and this had a comical effect. She also knew how to pronounce 'Sacheverell' Sitwell properly, one of the many names she dropped. Ma thought she was fun, but Aunty Dorothy disparaged Mary for her 'unnatural' dislike of children – 'can't stand the ghastly creatures', Mary Gaynor would exclaim.

There were things Ma didn't approve of – women shouldn't talk too much in front of men, she believed, because it takes away from a woman's 'mystery'. Oh tosh, I'd think. She didn't approve of divorce, but neither did most people in her generation – divorcees were not admitted to the Royal Enclosure at Ascot until 1968.

I'm not sure if Ma disliked divorce because it was unromantic or because she felt it left women worse off. Or because the Catholic catechism iterated that 'what God hath joined together, let no man pull asunder.' But then again, she was willing to make exceptions if she thought someone was charming enough or glamorous enough. She made an exception for the twice-divorced Mrs Wallis Simpson, whom she regarded as far more of a template for feminism than Mrs Pankhurst. To capture a king's heart was a far greater achievement, in Ma's eyes, than to go on demonstrations for the vote, which she honestly thought didn't matter a damn, as the same people with political 'pull' always seemed to get into power anyway, just taking turns to exercise their dominance.

Ma was an inconsistent person because she was such a romantic. She had grown up at Kilconnell, near Ballinasloe in Galway and her two heros were Galwegian men, but this pair couldn't have been more different. One was Liam Mellows, the left-wing Sinn Féin and IRA fighter – he believed in the abolition of all private property, like the Soviets – who was executed by the Free State in 1922. The other was the Earl of Clancarty, who was the local Anglo-Irish landlord in the Kilconnell area. But what these men had in common was – romance.

Liam Mellows had the romance of being the total idealist, who sacrificed his life for his ideals – dying for Ireland. The Earl of Clancarty had married a chorus girl – the beautiful Belle Bilton of the Empire Theatre, who was never accepted by the Ascendency. Mark Bence-Jones (in his peerless *Twilight of the Ascendency*) tells us that 'to relieve the tedium of life in her husband's rather austere mansion in County Galway she would drive into the nearby town of Ballinasloe and dazzle the inhabitants with the elegance of her turn-out.' It was a love-match and the Countess was beautiful and elegant. She was also, like her husband, extravagant, and the pair came to the verge of bankruptcy. Then, presently, the beautiful Lady Clancarty developed breast cancer and her devoted husband nursed her himself until the end – and mourned her for the rest of his life. It had remained a love-match! Ma thought this was an enchanting story, and retained great affection for the Earl of Clancarty (and Liam Mellows equally, to be sure).

If Ma was a romantic – and often witty – Aunty Dorothy was utterly practical and down-to-earth. My mother's advice about getting married was two-fold: 'Never let the sun go down on your anger', and 'never give a man bad news on an empty stomach.'

Aunty Dorothy's advice about marriage was, you might say, shrewder. 'When you get married, Mary,' she'd say, 'your attitude to your husband's assets should be: "what's thine is mine, but what's mine is my own".' She firmly believed a husband should support his wife; she also believed that the wife's dowry – which was still a fact of life in the County Tipperary of her childhood – was hers to dispose of.

Not that she was ever less than kind-hearted, materially. She was always generous, and gave in a methodical way to charities – to the Irish Society for the Prevention of Cruelty to Children, and to an animals' protection league called Our Dumb Friends. She gave, I think, most munificently to a campaign to stop Irish horses being exported to the Continent horsemeat, which was a very hot topic of the early to middle 1950s – generating much more discussion and controversy than the diktats, say, of the draconian Archbishop of Dublin, John Charles McQuaid, which were regarded rather as the way the weather was regarded: permanent and the cause of much eye-rolling.

Aunty Dorothy didn't approve of the French, because of their predilection for eating horse-flesh. She condemned their reputation for being fond of food by saying – 'they made a god of their belly.' I later discovered that this was an old Cromwellite prejudice against the pleasures of the table.

So there they were, the two mother-figures of my childhood, with completely different influences: one romantic and poetic, devoted to Oscar Wilde and to Goldsmith's 'The Deserted Village', her favourite poem. One down-to-earth and practical, knowledgeable about the domestic arts, about gardening and stately homes and even sport, which she followed avidly on TV. Aunty Dorothy was not uncultivated, but she was not a person for books. I am not sure if she ever read a book – I certainly never saw her read one, save for a catalogue about roses. She went so far as to condemn books and people who read books over-much – 'always got their nose stuck in a book'. She thought it heinous to spend time reading during fine weather. 'Get out and enjoy the sunshine, not stuck inside with your nose in a book.' I was allowed to borrow two books a week from the Ballsbridge Children's Library. When, on one occasion, I came home with three books, she made me take one back. It was the principle.

Aunty Dorothy could be also be liberal, although not always in a liberal-sounding way. She indicated in a subtle way that she endorsed of birth control – especially, she implied, for the tinkers, who had far too many children. She was philo-Semitic – pointing out to me that David Jacobs, of whom she was a great fan, the host of Juke Box Jury, was Jewish, and that accounted for his charm and knowledge of music, and it was wicked for people to be anti-Jewish. She also loved Danny Kaye and was delighted to announce that he was Jewish. However, she couldn't bring herself to warm to black Africans. 'Their lips are too big!' she'd cry. Then she didn't have the benefit of a convent education where they taught you all about the 'black babies' that Irish nuns and priests were educating on the missions, and the black babies were perfect dotes.

Aunty Dorothy had compassion for drunks and gamblers because she had had a male cousin, Garnet, who had been great fun, but who had turned rather raffish with the drink and the horses. Interestingly, she feared for the moral formation of boys more than of girls, and would issue dire warnings about the dangers of turning into 'a ne'er do well'. Her most dismissive words were for a lad who seemed as though he might become 'a ne'er do'.

Both of these women exercised an influence over me, and I can see the effect to this day.

And here's a strange thing. When I became a young feminist I railed against the dominance of men in public life. This was called the rule of the patriarchy. And of course when I was growing up, it certainly seemed as though men ruled the exterior world: men were in all the important positions, from politicians to ecclesiastics, from policemen – yes, the Ban Gardaí were launched during the mid-1950s, but they were never, in those days, in senior positions – to judges. And yet, if I think of the real influences on my character, and in my home life, it was women. My brothers were around, of course, and I loved them. My uncle Jim really did look after me – he paid the school bills, and most of the other bills too, and he took a hand in the discipline too. But the home was ruled by women, and the social norms were largely set by women, and I now think it is dishonest to ascribe all power in the past to men, because women always exercised what is called 'soft power', and some women exercised it to a domineering degree.

My childhood was odd – but then I was odd – and I have great regrets that I didn't get a better education, academically. Perhaps if Ritalin had been invented – to address my ADHD – I might have settled down and learned what I needed to learn, and thus achieved more intellectually. But regrets are pointless, and in life you just have to try and make the best of the hand you've been dealt – and that includes the kind of personality bestowed upon you by birth, genetic inheritance, and environment.

Yet I look back on the Dublin of my childhood as a kindly place, tolerant of eccentrics, and a place peopled by a range of characters who represented every part of the human spectrum.

My old home in Herbert Road is now part of the Sandymount Hotel, and it was flatteringly brought to my attention recently that their publicity leaflets make that very point. Mary Kenny grew up here. Just fancy.

Farewell, My Darling Sister

I think I had begun to know, by Christmas of 2002, that my sister's life was beginning to ebb away. But for a long time I was in denial, and chose to believe that she was in remission from the cervical cancer that had come to light in the spring of 2002. She did, indeed, make a brief recovery, but it was all too brief.

Ursula lived in New York City, where she had gone in the 1960s. She had been married, and she and Stefan had been happy for some years, but the marriage ended and her former husband had remarried in France. Since the 1990s, she had been alone, and for about ten years our relations were strained. We quarrelled bitterly on the day of our mother's funeral, in 1991: she called me hard-boiled and egotistical, I called her self-absorbed and neurotic.

Ursula was single, childless, living in Manhattan. I was married, with two sons, and living that frantic life of a working mother, in London. She thought my life was emotionally comfortable and secure – she saw England as a cosy place where the NHS provided for your health and nothing was never too tough or competitive. I thought her life was free from the responsibilities of having to rush around the supermarket at the end of a working day, free to explore the stimulus and openness of America.

Sibling rivalry is said to exist between sisters, and Ursula would have had good cause to resent a younger sibling. My parents initially had two sons, and then a daughter, Ursula. With that, the family seemed complete. My father adored Ursula, and for the first ten-and-a-half years of her life she had that unique father-daughter link. And then, greatly to everyone's surprise, and perhaps some embarrassment, I appeared. Suddenly, this surprise new baby was the focus of all eyes, and an over-robust aunt –

thinking only to tease – said to little Ursula: 'Now, whose nose is put out of joint! Now, who's no longer Daddy's little girl!'

Yet, almost my first memories are of Ursula caring for me, and looking after me. My mother always seemed to be busy doing something else, and was, in any event, bored by childcare: it was Ursula who bathed me, washed my hair, dressed me nicely and babysat me. I remember so well when she would put a bandage on my knee after a scrape, first cleaning the scratch with iodine, and saying tenderly – 'Now be a brave soldier.' I still say that to myself when facing an ordeal.

We didn't have our first quarrel until I was a boisterous teenager – by which time she was in her mid-twenties. Ursula was quiet, thoughtful, artistic and pretty; I was noisy, brawney, extrovert, and a handful.

The years scrolled by. Throughout our adult lives we were always in touch, and sometimes very close. She loved America, and insisted on my coming to New York in the 1960s, where I stayed in the Upper East Side apartment she shared with her best friend, Liz Nohilly. Ursula loved buying me clothes and little gifts; she wanted me to be chic and glamorous, instead of eccentrically bohemian, but she was soft and indulgent, never sharply critical. The rift came when she thought I no longer had time for her; this wasn't so, but the time available to a working mother can be frenetically rationed.

In 2002, she was diagnosed with cancer. Ursula had long been a devotee of Chinese herbs, and she placed too much faith in them when she was first unwell. The herbalist showed a dereliction of duty, in my opinion, by not advising her to go to a conventional doctor. I now wonder if she held back from visiting an ordinary doctor because of the expense. A doctor's visit could cost, in Manhattan, $300. She did have some insurance, but you still have to pay to see a physician initially.

She eventually had surgery and radiation and the cancer was pronounced 'contained'. Her New York friends were wonderful, and her former husband, Stefan, very kind, retaining a real devotion to Ursula. She had a happy trip to France, where she visited Lourdes, as she desired. But by Christmas of 2002, she was beginning to fail.

She shielded me from the truth for as long as possible. I was working on a book that involved visiting Germany and she held back from revealing her situation until it was impossible to disguise it any more. In March she called me on the mobile: I was sitting in my car outside the Imperial War Museum. She just said that from now on it was 'palliative care only', then broke down and rang off. I just sat there, stunned, for a very long time.

Between March and June, I made five trips to New York, my stomach churning each time I boarded that transatlantic aircraft, terrified of how I would find her: each time a little thinner and more sepulchral, yet each time sweeter and kinder and more loving to me. This need to mother me lasted right up to the end. When she was dying, at the Cabrini Hospice in East 19th Street, she sent me off to a Fifth Avenue sale, so that I should have three Lord & Taylor embroidered nighties, marked down to $17.50. They are so pretty, and I think of her each time I take them out.

After she died, I found scores of letters she had written to various business connections in America in which she sought to promote a book I had written about Ireland in 1997. The generosity with which she described my modest efforts moved me to painful feelings of regret that, really, I never did show her my full appreciation of all she had done for me. And although I spent time with her in the last months of her life, there was something cowardly in my attitude: I still pretended death was not imminent.

She died surrounded by many, many friends – Americans are very generous and often in a practical way: New York friends would visit, with chicken soup and a fistfuls of dollars, to help with the costs of drugs. Ursula was spiritual, and she was much consoled by the comforts of religion. She had the priest, a wonderful gospel minister named Joseph, a visiting Rabbi, who told an Irish joke which made everyone smile, and, at the end, a Zen Buddhist carer who literally helps people to die, Randy Phillips. The Zen philosophy is that to understand life, you must understand the importance of letting go. And you must live in each day, savouring every minute, not projecting into the future or fretting over the past.

But after she breathed her last, I went back to her apartment, and sat among her possessions, all touched with the soft perfume of her personality, and just howled. Nothing can comfort us for loss, for remembrance of things past, for the knowledge that never again will I dial that Manhattan code, 212, and hear her voice.

I think of her most often at airports. I remember how I would call her on departing from Newark, or JFK, and she'd be so concerned that everything was all right for me, even when she herself was dying. I'd ring off with the words 'Be back soon, darling sis', but in that sense, I will never be back: for it was not I, but my beloved sister, who was preparing to depart, for all time.

I'll never stop missing her, sometimes at the most unexpected moments. Sitting at a drinks bar at Heathrow Airport in 2009, opening *The New Yorker*, which she loved, I'd remember and dissolve into tears. *Be a brave soldier*. She was.

* * *

Ursula's poem, given to me by her Turkish friend Muhsine at Listowel. Muhsine has translated it into Turkish and published it in a Turkish magazine. It was written during one of our periods of estrangement but evokes, indeed, something of myself.

Illusion?

Sad, how I now count her
With the departed ones
For whom I pray and I mourn.

She, Shirley Temple child
Artful, wanton and pagan-wise
Once in my love-dipped heart I'd borne.

She who I loved above all
(save for a few)
She who bedazzled I watched
As performer she grew.

She who seemed angel yet ever so human kin
Courageously clever and funny and raised above sin.

When, and why, and where and how did it end
Maybe too few deeds…and too many words were penned
Too many coarse and careless acts will finally freeze
The most eager heart's flow and cause it to seize.

Was it, I wonder, all from her first childhood start
A perfectly wistful illusion on my part?

Ursula Kenny
13 October 1992

The Reluctant Carer

Those who are family carers – individuals who care for a sick or disabled spouse, parent, child or sibling – are often called 'saintly', and indeed I can think of some who truly are saints. I have been called 'saintly' myself, in this role, but I know well that I am no saint, and that caring can be done freely, voluntarily, and even willingly – but, at the same time, there can be anger, resentment, frustration and even a tragic feeling that one's own life is being eaten away.

A dear friend of mine, Mavis Arnold, cared devotedly for her elderly mother, who lived to a great age. No daughter could have done more, and Mavis looked after her mother in her own home in County Dublin. Towards the end of the old lady's life – which turned out to be very long – Mavis said: 'What I worry about – will there be any time left over for me?' There wasn't a lot. A few short years after her mother died, Mavis herself became afflicted by Alzheimer's, and has been cared for, very devotedly, by her husband Bruce.

But that is what the carer thinks, even in the midst of ministrations: 'will there be any time left over for me?' That is what I ponder all the time.

The thought came to me, that after my husband's death, I might write a description of being his carer, just to put an account on the record, as honestly as I could. More and more people are carers for spouses, and other family members, and more and more people in the future, will be carers, because the elderly population is growing. Then gradually, another thought came to me: perhaps I would not outlive my husband – despite his being more than fourteen years older than me, and despite his being ever more crippled from a stroke. ('Crippled' is not considered a kind word nowadays, but it is a truthful word. He cannot walk or do anything much for himself, except perhaps lift a cup of tea with the one remaining operational arm.) I have seen people live in wheelchairs for years, being seriously disabled; and I have seen healthy and energetic individuals sicken and die overnight. 'I'm sorry your husband is poorly,' sympathisers remark. 'He's not poorly – he's quite healthy,' I explain. 'He is just disabled – he has no mobility.'

But – 'will there be any time left over for me?' That is my Hamlet-like question, and one that has convinced me I must leave a testament of a carer's experience.

* * *

It was September 1996, and my cousin Brendan O'Reilly was getting married – to his French fiancée Martine – in the Bordeaux region, and the immediate family and the various cousins were all travelling to France for the wedding. My husband, Richard West, chose not to come along with me and our two sons, but that was not unusual.

Dick (as he was always called in the family, Richard, more formally) and I, who were married in 1974, were never a hugger-mugger, couple-dom-couple. We were reasonably happy together – all marriages have uneven bits, but there were many good times. Yet it was a marriage of two independently-minded people. I practised the feminist principle of autonomy – it didn't worry me at all to go anywhere on my own, be it a theatre, a restaurant, a trip (my children thought me 'weird' because I actually preferred going to the cinema alone), and he had never been a great one for family gatherings. There was an annual get-together of his very amiable West cousins every summer, and I don't think he attended it once. He liked his cousins – and the clan included the brilliant actor Timothy West, his first cousin – but family gatherings were just not his gig.

Social occasions Dick would only join under duress – he did accompany me, twice, to 10 Downing Street when Margaret Thatcher invited me for a soirée, though his reasoning was that this was a duty associated with journalistic work. He was an affable host on his own patch – he'd be warmly welcoming to people who came to visit us when we lived in a flat in Holland Park, Kensington, from 1981 to 1997, but loathed being dragged along to any kind of a sit-down meal. I learned, after some years of fiascos, that pressurising Dick into dinner parties usually meant it would end in disaster, somehow. I'd prefer to go alone – not to have the responsibility of trying to make it agreeable for him.

He liked Brendan and Martine, but he'd sooner meet up those he liked in a pub, because, as he explained many times, a pub gives a man freedom to come and go as he pleases. There are no social obligations in a pub. You meet someone, you share a pint, you leave whenever you choose: the sociability of freedom and independence. In his days of travelling as a foreign correspondent, Dick might come and go from a London pub and the next thing he'd be in Vietnam, or another favourite destination, Port Moresby in Papua New Guinea. (When I was sorting through his papers during one of our several house moves, I found a letter from Claire Tomalin, writing to him back in the 1970s: 'Oh Dick – where are you? You were in the Bunghole [then the New Statesman watering hole] only five minutes ago!') The most frequent epistolary plea, from his friends and family alike was: 'Where are you, Dick? Write to us!'

So attending a wedding in the Bordeaux region without my husband was just fine. If he didn't feel like joining a family gathering, that's the way it often was. My sons would be with me, as would my niece Marie-Louise, along with her mother, May, and my cousin Geraldine and her husband, Keith, who were all good company. And French weddings are celebrated with brio, so the occasion was all very jolly.

This was the era before the mobile phone was ubiquitous, so I'm not sure how the message reached me, since I wasn't staying at a hotel, but with friends of Martine, my cousin's fiancée. But some network was activated, and I was told to telephone London. And thus did I discover that Dick had had a stroke. My friend Marjorie Wallace was helping out (as was one of Dick's oldest pals, Corinna Adam), but I should return to London pronto. It wasn't, I was informed, a serious stroke, but it was a stroke just the same, and Dick was on his way to hospital.

I remember receiving the news in a public telephone box on a balmy day in Bordeaux, while the city trams cruised by. And I remember, too, my reaction to it. I walked through the streets of Bordeaux, looking at antequarian bookshop windows and my thoughts were probably less than saintly. I was told he was 'comfortable' and 'not in danger'. But, I wondered, will he make a full recovery or will I now have to step into the position of being a full-time nurse? I vowed that my life was not going to be taken over by this situation: I had had a struggle to build and maintain a career, to keep it going through all challenges, and now, at the age of fifty-two and the children grown up – elder son nearly twenty-two, younger son eighteen – I wanted to expand as a writer, to travel more, to learn more, do more, not be tied down to an invalid husband.

I was aware that these were selfish thoughts, but a writer is an ego-driven animal, not a saintly, surrendered wife who puts everyone else first. A writer puts the writing first. Moreover, I had been one of the founders of a women's liberation movement which affirmed a woman's entitlement to her own fulfillment, and her right to freedom from the traditional forms of female oppression – domesticity, self-sacrifice for the sake of the care of others, the martyrdom of saintly altruism. I had been attracted to feminism and 'women's liberation' so as to escape the fate of my mother and my aunt – tied to the kitchen sink and the role of domestic organiser. Was I now to be drawn back into that realm?

And so I made my way back to London. Marjorie noted tartly, years later, that I didn't hurry unduly, since we travelled back to England overland, via Paris, by the same route we had gone. Still, I didn't do what my own instinct might have prompted me to do: take the first plane to Port Moresby.

Dick was ensconced in St Mary's Hospital, Paddington, and he seemed to be well looked after. The stroke had indeed been quite slight, with a mild effect on his left arm, for which he was due some physiotherapy. Pals and colleagues visited – Charles Moore, Tony Howard, Corinna Adam, Geoffrey Wheatcroft – and, so far as I recall, he seemed cheerful. Things weren't too bad: he'd take drugs to help his blood pressure and perhaps it would just be a little episode he would surmount. Life resumed, more or less, but not wholly, as before. The left arm had lost mobility, and there was a slight limp, too, on the left side.

The following year, 1997, he was resolved to leave London and settle in a quiet town by the seaside. When he was researching a book about

Chaucer, he found such a town, by the name of Deal, eight miles from Dover, nineteen miles from Canterbury. It was a pleasing little seaside place, with a touch of bohemianism: journalists and writers, we were told, often came to live there. The usual explanation was that journos would totter to Charing Cross from Fleet Street and fall asleep on the train, waking at Deal. I was dismayed, at first, by how long the train journey took, from London – over two hours. I suggested we might as well settle in France, and we looked at some houses on the enchanting Côte d'Opale, at Wimereux. But somehow Deal won out. We departed Holland Park on the day of Princess Diana's funeral in 1997. I mourned for London for many years afterwards ,and even held on to my precious residents' parking permit for Chelsea and Kensington for ages. A golden disc that allows the bearer to park in Sloane Street!

* * *

And so the years passed, and life went on. But gradually, in small measures, but unmistakably, Richard's mobility deteriorated, affecting first the left leg and the subsequently paralysed left arm. We went to Portugal on holiday in 1999 and I realised how his walking was slowing down: he began to lean on me rather more, physically as well as metaphorically. The intimacies of marriage were changing too. (I phoned my sister, lamenting 'My sex life has come to an end!' Heartlessly, but not unfairly, she retorted: 'Well, you've had a good run for your money!')

I had to help him a little more with everything. He became nervous about stepping into the shower, so that I had to stand by and make sure he would be safe. Richard never was a domesticated man, but there were certain domestic tasks he would and could do: bring me a cup of tea or coffee, and go out for the newspapers each morning. By the turn of the century, although he could still walk (and accomplished an impressive stretch by the Deal seashore, with our friends Julie and Joe Steeples, for the dawn of 2000), he became more apprehensive about his balance and couldn't walk without a stick. He had to have a kind of satchel strapped around his shoulders to bring back the morning papers, and then he couldn't go for the mornng papers any more.

Old age is loss. Little by little, you let go of what you once had. A stroke creeps over the body in a physical illumination of that process.

The first decade of the twenty-first century contained many melancholy events for me: there were wrenching losses in my family in Ireland, and a distressing number of my friends and contemporaries died in their fifties and sixties, some chronicled in this volume. My oldest London friend, Miriam Polunin, died aged fifty-nine, killed by an arsonist who maliciously set fire to her mother's home in Cheshire when Miriam was visiting. My musician friend, Clare Cole, who had many associations with Westminster Cathedral, died from breast cancer before she was sixty, forever smiling; Jenny Floyd, whose children had so often spent time with mine, died from liver disease – literally overnight in her early sixties. My Ballybunion friend and *Irish Times* colleague, Mary Cummins, died in 1999 from lung cancer, in her late fifties. My former agent, Maggie Noach, a woman in her fifties, went into a private hospital for an investigation about persistant back pain, was informed that she needed a surgical intervention to correct her back, and died from a massive heart attack during the operation. My beloved sister, here chronicled – along with others – died in 2003, and my darling niece Sarah, from a brain tumour in 2007. There were other losses too; death and decay and decline I seemed to see all around.

It is normal to notice the thinning of the ranks with age. There is a juncture in life when you start going to many more funerals than to weddings or christenings. But I didn't expect to see this occur so soon. In my generation, we were confidently informed that we'd be living so much longer than our parents and grandparents, and with so much better health and medical care, we could expect to live well into our eighties. But so many of my friends and contemporaries were dying before their sixtieth birthday, and well before their seventieth. And this, of course, had the effect of making me contemplate my own death. How much longer would I have? How many more Sundays would I spend cooking and feeding and washing up and generally serving a husband who could do less and less for himself? 100? 300? 500? A spouse who is a carer has to do more than twice the usual home chores: the duties associated with care, and all the other household responsibilities as well.

I recently wrote a job description of what a carer's role involves, sometimes on a daily basis: Meals and household chores. Personal care. Laundry. Shopping and cooking. Dealing with household maintenance and adaptations. Dental monitoring. Pharmaceutical and medical. Scratching – invalids can suffer from tormenting itches and can't reach to scratch. Chiropody and chiropody arrangements. Hair washing and cutting arrangements. Valeting. Administrative paperwork – bills, cheques, bank statements, solicitors' correspondence, invoices, remittances (the carer becomes the caree's attorney). Social and therapeutic support. 'Toilet issues', including bowel monitoring. Grooming issues – doing the manicure of the caree. Pensions and tax. Recreation – taking out, etc, or arranging outings. Technical maintenance (phones, lifelines, etc.) Companionship. Providing reading matter or reading aloud. Transportation. Holiday plans, if applicable. Passports and similar. Money management. Disability vehicle fixer. Eye care – spectacles. Dealing with local authority issues. Managing extra carers and help. *Et cetera.*

This was not how I planned to spend my fifties and sixties, sometimes called, optimistically, 'the harvest years'. I thought I would have more freedom, more leisure, and the chance to spend time in libraries, at cinemas, in theatres, pursuing research, travelling. I watched other contemporaries – often couples – talk merrily about taking crusies hither and thither, flying off to holiday hotspots, Turkey, the Canaries, having canal holidays in France; but any holiday plans involved my taking care of a husband less and less able to do anything for himself.

We had a brief time in the south of Spain in the autumn of 2003, near Seville, but this was also the beginning of The Falls. As his legs were growing weaker, Dick would lose his balance and fall. The Falls became a source of unrelenting anxiety. The fear had started in a Spanish hotel, where the distance from the bathroom to the bed seemed, to Richard, vast, and without wall or furniture support, for he had learned to do 'furniture walking' – holding on to pieces of furniture as he progressed, and the polished wood floor seemed to him like an ice rink. Was I blamed for choosing that hotel in that place? I felt responsible, anyway.

Again, at the beginning of The Falls, he would manage to get on his feet again, and I was able to help him. I'd stand over him while he'd pick his way, with such trepidation, from the living room to the downstairs loo, leaning on the furniture as he went. There was talk of a stairlift, but the medical advice was that he should go on walking for as long as he could: 'use it, or lose it'.

I'd then watch him gingerly step into the shower. Every step had to be carefully calculated, and sometimes attempted five, ten, fifteen times – one foot forward and then, in fear of a fall, back again. One foot forward, and then back again, again. However cautious each step was, it was still a provisional step: it could lead to collapse at any moment. At one point, in 2009, I noticed that his lower body was purple with bruises. An observer might have thought him a victim of domestic violence, but it was – only – the result of The Falls: falls in the bedroom, on the lavatory, in the hall. I'd notice how much more frail his legs had become, putting every ounce of energy into each faltering step.

I would dread, then, The Thud: the sound when he fell, either from bed or when trying to walk. His own response was often admirably patient and stoical. He wouldn't complain, just lie there trying to get himself up, or waiting until I got him up, or, if our son Patrick was in the house, both of us could often manage to do so, although it could take an hour and a mighty number of heaves. Sometimes the paramedics had to be called to raise Richard from the floor.

Almost wittily, he remarked one day that he felt like the character in Kafka's *Metamorphosis*, when a man wakes up one morning changed into a beetle, lying athwart his beetle's back, unable to rise – a surreal story (sometimes interpreted as a metaphor of being Jewish in an anti-Semitic culture) which is nonetheless startlingly believable. Dick felt like that man who had become a beetle, his helpless little limbs waving in the air.

Leaving the house – especially if Richard were alone – became more and more problematic. I tried to maintain the habit of spending a few days of every month in Dublin, and, one way and another I am grateful that I have been able to do that: but from 2004 onwards, there was always a worry about The Falls, and there had to be someone on hand to make sure he was all right. We began to have home helpers who would look in to check him, and male helpers who would assist him to the shower. We also had very good Deal friends in Joe and Julie Steeples, Chrissy and the late Peter

Birkett, Colin and Josephine Whittington, and Carole and Dave Hubble, as well as other helpful neighbours. But on several occasions Dick asked me not to leave him, and I cancelled trips. I cancelled visits to London, too, and more reluctantly, to Paris – a non-refundable Eurostar booking. But could I have enjoyed Paris if overcome by the guilt of abandoning him?

I did get to Paris in 2008, and my cousin Brendan said to me, when I described the situation: 'It can only get worse.' He was being truthful, but the phrase made me miserable: 'It can only get worse.' And indeed, it did.

* * *

From around the period when The Falls began in earnest – from the autumn of 2003 – I became subjected to cyclical episodes of crashing depressions. I would not describe myself as a depressive person: everyone has ups and downs, but I am normally reasonably resilient. But circum- stances now sent me into that often-described black pit. During these episodes, all I could see around me was darkness, and a feeling of being low, low, low down in that pit. Weekends were the worst: I would experi- ence this draining sensation, as if everything in my body was at a low ebb, every particle of energy being sucked away, like an ebbing tide on a shore.

One day, in the spring of 2004 – around the time I turned sixty – while driving between Deal and Tunbridge Wells, the thought came to me that I could fake a car crash, and end my life, right here, right now. A faked car crash, which involves no one else, is a known way of taking your own life. The thought began to dominate my consciousness and I had to take deep breaths to eliminate it. Deep breath and count to ten: turn on the radio: deep breath and count to ten. A programme came on the radio presented by a friend of ours, Andrew Brown. Concentrate on Andrew Brown, and his interesting descriptions of Sweden. Deep breath. I could end this mis- ery right here, right now. Deep breath. It's a sin. It causes untold sorrow for those left behind. Deep breath.

The terrible, crazy, frightening moment passed, but since it struck I have identified with those who do take their own lives, when sunk in depression. You have to stand against suicide: a society has to try and discourage it, because it causes so much grief. And it is wrong to give the signal that it is just another 'choice', because only a childless orphan living on a desert island could make such a choice without affecting others. But when that profound despair hits, the idea will always occur. It presents itself as a way out, a final blanking out of all the misery.

My GP, who has always been terrifically helpful, offered me anti-depressants when I mentioned these moments of despair, but I declined because I felt that the problem wasn't one of mood, or a chemical imbalance that can be corrected by a pharmaceutical solution. The problem lay in my circumstances. I remember a famous advert for Valium featured in the medical journals back in the 1960s, which showed a photo of a young mother with a small child, living in an ugly concrete high-rise tower block. The selling slogan said – 'You can't change her circumstances, but you can change her mood.'

There may be circumstances when it is appropriate to get help with changing a mood – geriatric conditions might be one – but I didn't want my mood changed, I wanted a solution to the problem of my life circumstances. I was unhappy because I felt so dreadfully trapped. This was how I would spend the rest of my days: as a carer to an invalid husband, in a small seaside town in England, which, though it might have kindly people, was not my choice of location. Sometimes I'd play the old mournful music of the Irish exile on a CD, and wallow in a sense of loneliness and alienation: 'The Old Bog Road', 'Raglan Road', 'Dublin in the Rare Auld Times'. If only I could be in Dublin in the Rare Auld Times!

If I could just change the circumstances, the depressions would lift, I believed. And of course, I could change the circumstances temporarily: I could get more help with minding Dick, and escape, for brief interludes. And when I did, I came to feel that the most beautiful phrase in the English language was: 'This train is now departing for Charing Cross.' Even the automated announcements formed themselves into poetry:

> *This train is now departing for Charing Cross*
> *Change at Dover for Continental links –*
> *Change at Ashford for the Eurostar*
> *To Paris, Brussels, and Lille.*
> *This train is now departing for Charing Cross . . .*
> *For a destination of Liberty!*

* * *

And how about Richard himself? How did he take the involuntary change in his own life circumstances? The alteration from being a man of independence and even detachment from bourgeois and domestic life – his greatest fulfilment, during his active life, came with travelling and writing – to dependence, increased disability, falling, and indeed pain?

Looking back, it was at first so gradual that he didn't seem too unhappy. Between 1996 and 2003, his life was manageable, even if there was decline. The eternal wanderer actually became more domesticated, and certainly more uxorious: now we really were entwined in coupledom. I remember picking him up from an outpatient hospital appointment, and noting the look of thankfulness, recognition and relief in his eyes as he spotted me approaching him. I had seldom seen that look in our salad days – merriment, laughter, pleasure, yes, but not gratitude and relief for my presence, as though I were the lifeguard saving the swimmer at risk of drowning.

He enjoyed reading and watching nature programmes on TV and seeing friends at a lovely local pub in Deal, the Prince Albert, run by an adorably kind couple, Michael Harlick and Colin Vurley, who were also friends. In our prime, we had both (alas) been heavy drinkers: I was an alcoholic vixen, Dick more a regular boozer who sometimes did so excessively (his excuse, which indeed was plausible, was that he was too shy to do a journalistic job without a few drinks: where I, he said, was 'perfectly effervescent' while sober, and a termagant when drunk). I quit drinking, thankfully, in 1991 – best change I ever made – and after his stroke, Dick moderated greatly. But the pint of real ale was a genuine pleasure to him, especially at the Prince Albert.

But even the trip to the pub began to become an obstacle course – staggering to the door of the pub even before he had had a single drink; through the door only with the help of two men. Then it all began to close in and less and less was possible. Dick himself went through cycles of anger, cycles of grumpiness, and then times of laughter again. His sense of humour has never deserted him, and neither has the stoicism that was bred into him by the English formation of the stiff upper lip. 'Mustn't grumble.' 'Don't make a fuss.' And the immortal: 'Keep Calm and Carry On.' But he could be bad-tempered. On one occasion, when we were having a meal with friends at a local restaurant, he told me, with a flash of hostility, that I had a 'witch's laugh'. (I do cackle a bit, 'tis true.) He believed, anyway, that I was bossy, and would revert to his Chaucerian theme that women seek 'maistery' (mastery). But someone has to make decisions and get things done!

One day I said to him – 'Do you think I'd have been a more fulfilled person if I'd gone to Oxford – or Trinity College Dublin?' (I left school at sixteen and am very chippy about it.)

'No,' he replied. 'Because you are a discontented person. You would always be discontented.' Maybe so, I reflected, although discontent is surely the soil of ambition.

He had more vehement bursts of anger when I would be the object of that ire (he'd accuse me, with some justice, of being such a clutterbug that I had ruined every home I'd dwelt in). I understood this: Dr Johnson says, somewhere, that a spouse will always be the first to take the flak when an individual is angry – just because they are there. I didn't mind the anger, because I shared it, perhaps, and I admired his stoicism and acceptance of circumstances when he was in that mode.

What I minded was the ever-growing passivity, and the way in which I was responsible for everything. If we were to go out to a meal, or even the pub, I'd have to bring the car around, get Dick into the car, drive to the location, get him out of the car and into the restaurant or bar, sit him down, order a drink, then go and park the car and return. As we were near France, we could go to St Omer for lunch or dinner and come back the same day, and I would have to do everything – money, passports, and subsequently, wheelchair arrangements, driving arrangements, and all the driving and motor car maintenance. I also frequently paid, as I was earning more than him, though money was something we never quarrelled about or even divvied up in any particular way: whoever had the cash, paid.

But there was no other way of going anywhere, unless I arranged it, and passers-by would sometimes lend a hand. But my role was minding Dick, and it weighed upon me.

Old couples can get crabby with one another anyway. One day I was talking about painting (the unspoken message being that I missed not being able to get to the National Gallery or the Royal Academy, being stuck in Deal looking after him) and the nineteenth-century pictures in the Tate. 'I always like narrative pictures,' I said. 'Yes, you do,' he replied, in a dissenting tone.

'You don't really like my taste in pictures, do you?'

'No, not really.'

'You don't like my taste in poetry, much, either, do you?'

'No, not a lot.'

'In fact, we've nothing in common, really. You've no interest in the theatre. You don't like anything I like.'

'No, I suppose not.'

A long pause. Then he says: 'But I love you just the same!'

I laugh, and say – 'On cue! It took a moment, but you got there!'

Later, as we were getting into bed, I said, wearily, thinking of a number of worries:

'Oh, well, we'll be dead soon, and that will solve all the problems.'

'Yes,' he said, good-humouredly. 'But *not soon enough!*'

* * *

Although outwardly, you are, as a carer, performing all these responsible duties and apparently devoted to someone else, inwardly being a carer can also make you self-centred. 'Will there be any life left over for me?' is the haunting refrain that lingers over each day. You begin to feel you have given so much of yourself to the central issue of the caree's welfare that you have to conserve some little part left for yourself.

Deal has a lot of older people and although I was polite and reasonably kind – I hope – to elderly neighbours who were beginning to fail, I told myself I would not get seriously involved in any further elderly care: *one caree is enough*. We had a nice friend, Michael Hill – an amusing man who had worked for the BBC – who went to a care home, and I visited him once – possibly twice. But when one of his neighbours said to me in the supermarket – 'Do go and see Mike', I rebelled inwardly: *No! I'm not taking on another elderly person! One invalid eating up my last span of existence is enough!*

I told myself, 'I'm still entitled to a life'. If I had a cup of coffee in the kitchen before bringing one to Dick, I'd tell myself: 'I'm entitled to look after myself'. But I have to keep saying that to justify anything. 'I'm entitled to go to the cinema.' 'I'm entitled to a week's respite.'

Yet I have felt ashamed, often, of my own self-centred preoccupations, my solipsistic focus on how this was using up *my life*. In November 2005, I wrote in my diary: 'If I had any humanity, my heart would be full of pity and compassion for Dick: to watch him dress, so slowly and gingerly, like a child putting on its first clothes; to see him get to his feet, sometimes after two or three attempts; to see him walk, with faltering steps, from the bedroom to the bathroom; an old man for whom everything is an effort, and yet he has the character and the fortitude to do it all, to keep going because that is what you do. My heart should be consumed with pity, if I had real humanity. But I am in the position that Yeats described so well: 'Too long a sacrifice/Can make a stone of the heart'. My pity for him is stifled by the despair I feel about my own life. In 2010, I will be sixty-six. Will I still be rising each morning to attend to the kitchen, the laundry, the household chores, making breakfast and serving it to him, fetching the papers, facing a day squeezing journalistic deadlines into the interstices of housewifery and caring? Yes, I will, unless I change things.' But I wasn't able to change things; or I wasn't able to change the central thing, which was that I was *responsible*.

I would sometimes cook a meal for friends, noting that 'I entertain guests for the same reason as I would give children's parties for my kids when they were young: to ensure the kids had friends and a social life. Now it was to ensure Dick has a social life.' But as I peeled and chopped vegetables I would think: 'This is the way my life ebbs away – peeling carrots.' And deeply resenting it; full of duty and loathing.

The sense that this was to be a life sentence was growing on me. Friends quoted Richard Burton (the Arabist, not the movie star) who had written on his wall: 'This too will pass', but the coda, for me, would be 'yes, and so will I pass.' I would find some relief from writing mournful poetry – I composed a whole collection, darkly entitled *La Prisonniere*, being a lamentation in the form of free verse. (Alternative title: *The Fucking Kitchen Sink*.) I developed a nasty case of psoriasis, with blotchy patches of extreme eczema all over my arms, legs and buttocks. I also seemed to have a permanently upset stomach, and sometimes dreadful episodes of irritable bowel and nausea.

Dublin always was the great escape – the great respite – for me. I felt like kissing the ground, like the Pope, when I'd arrive at Dublin Airport, and when leaving, I felt all the lonesomeness of the Exile of Erin. The blue remembered hills girdled around my native city! The ghost of my late brother James at the airport gate . . .

Minding Dick, in Kent, a sense of exile from Ireland was sometimes acute. I'd think of the Irish countryside in the summer, elegiacally described in a great old balled which begins, 'I'm a freeborn man/ Of the travelling people . . .' Heaven, to me, seemed to me to be alighting from a train at Limerick Junction, the Galtee mountains all around, the crossing of the Shannon beckoning and the freshness of an Irish breeze upon which is borne the intoxicating scent of liberty.

My sense of rootedness in Ireland runs deep anyway, but there was another element in play: connecting with what I thought of as my true identity. In Kent, I felt myself to be defined as someone's carer, rather as some angry feminists have felt their identity was some man's daughter, some man's wife, some man's mother, but never themselves. Increasingly, my 'carer' identity became self-defining, and it was accompanied by a draining away of self-worth. The maddening English habit of strangers addressing older women with patronising endearments such as 'dearie', 'darlin', and 'my love' (while simultaneously addressing all men as 'sir') also felt so diminishing: I was just this old biddy whose only identity was as an unpaid carer.

I also blamed Dick, perhaps unfairly – I had, after all, agreed to the move – for decamping to Deal. It is an absolute fact that a journalist who leaves London gets less work. Forget all the eyewash about communications nowadays all being done by email and other electronic means: in journalism, what matters is (1) continuous personal connections and (2) proximity. When living in London, I had a regular amount of TV and radio work, but if you can't get to studios, you are literally not in the picture. I also missed my London friends terribly.

But when I went to Dublin, or Ireland generally, my identity was altogether different: there I saw myself as a working journalist, a competent professional woman who was treated as an independent adult – sometimes, even, with a certain esteem. My Irish identity was fulfilling and intellectually rich; my English life seemed repressed, petty and intellectually deprived. This also set up a tension which could trigger depressions.

And yes, my vanity and pride were dented by this role I had to take on. I remember the American feminist Gloria Steinem once writing that women were judged according to the kind of man who was escorting them (well, she was talking about sophisticated Manhattan in the 1960s and 1970s). The woman's status was rated, by the maitre d' at the upscale restaurant, according to the social standing of the guy she was with. (Men to whom I repeated this countered that a man was often judged according to the status of woman he was able to attract.) The point is that social judgements are made according to your role in life, and I mourned the loss of my life as an autonomous person and in my time a reasonably successful journalist. Then I'd reproach myself and feel guilty for the sin of pride. A proper Christian would welcome an opportunity to practise humility and to earn grace!

You'd think religious faith would buoy me up a little: it does and it doesn't. Religion often underlines the miseries of this life. 'Think,' said a Dublin friend, 'of the Book of Job!' The Biblical Psalms are replete with lamentations about what a valley of tears we dwell in. Jesus Christ said: 'Take up your Cross and follow me.' The Buddha's ruling principle is 'Life is Suffering'. Religion helped me to face this reality: yes, you're in a valley of tears – get used to it. Catholic guilt certainly propelled me to do my duty – without the urgings of Catholic guilt I might be inclined to walk away. Catholic guilt popped up to remind me of the sacramental marriage vows: 'For better, for worse, in sickness and in health, till death do us part.'

Religion helps you to contemplate that suffering; it doesn't promise you – not one bit – that your suffering will be alleviated or you will soon be liberated from it. You won't be. So get on your knees and pray for fortitude.

But faith does help you to reflect on the afflictions of others, and many people have great afflictions. I see mothers with handicapped children; mothers who have lost their children; friends struck down in their prime with chronic illness; friends with cancer, in their prime. A dear friend in

Dublin – a gifted writer and a matchless cook – contracted Parkinson's Disease at the age of sixty-four and her sufferings have been heroically borne. She too has been cared for, with the greatest tenderness, by her husband.

* * *

In 2010 we had what turned out to be a very difficult trip to Ireland. I drove all the way – a long way, too, all around the pesky M25 – from Deal to Dublin and then across Ireland to County Leitrim. I was invited to give a talk in Leitrim (at the Anthony Trollope Summer School, for Trollope owed his awakening as a writer to his time in Ireland), and I thought I might combine it with a holiday for Dick and myself. The previous year, we had gone for a week to northern France. It had been a struggle, but we had just about managed, with the help of a wheelchair, and the assistance of passers-by getting him in and out of the car.

The journey to the West of Ireland was desperately gruelling. There were endless falls, and it was altogether pitiful. The driving was laborious, and the help episodic. He was, by then, on his last legs. With heroic support – again, Patrick was able to be there some of the time – Richard was just about able to stand up, and to walk a few yards, but it was such hard labour for everyone. And sometimes, I'd leave him for a couple of hours in a hotel bedroom, and come back and find him, once more, on the floor. It really was a wretched experience. It was also the last time I was to see my remaining sibling, Carlos, alive. And yet I wasn't able to spend much time with Carlos because of my constant responsibility for Richard. We couldn't stay at my flat in Dublin because it would have been impossible to get a wheelchair into the lift, so we stayed at Bewley's Hotel in Ballsbridge, near where I grew up. The hotel could accommodate a wheelchair, but I can't say I found the general attitude of the staff particularly helpful. Nobody was exactly unkind, but there was a discernible detachment in attitudes towards this elderly invalid and his wife pushing a wheelchair. The attitude was, I felt, that it was my responsibility. It all seemed to cost so much, too.

On the return journey, at Chester, Richard asked if we could stay overnight at the railway hotel there. I took one look at the front, and its high Victorian façade, and knew we could never negotiate the steps. He was disappointed, and I reproach myself now for having to disappoint him: perhaps we could have tried, and someone would have carried him all the way? Richard always loved the old British Rail hotels. But he also had, and continues to have, an unrealistic assessment in his own mobility.

So we stayed the night, instead, at an accessible hotel in Northamptonshire, and he could barely put one foot in front of the other. That summer of 2010 was the last time in which he could, in some manner, and with much support, get to his feet.

Gradually, gradually, decline, decline, decline: the legs seizing up, the bad arm ever more paralysed. By the autumn of 2010, it was sometimes taking me ninety minutes to get him showered, and there were increasing difficulties in managing the toilet. Sometimes he'd need to get up two or three times during the night, and I would, of course, get up with him to ensure he didn't fall. Even so, sometimes he did fall. And then in that late autumn there was a serious fall, an absolute and final fall.

It was 2.45 in the morning in our small terraced house in Deal, when Dick suddenly fell to the floor, from bed. There was the awful thud. And then silence. He lay stunned for a few moments, not answering my calls to him: 'Dick – are you all right?' He was momentarily unconscious but he hadn't changed colour, rolled his eyes or vomited, the classic signs of concussion. I called the ambulance. The paramedics quickly arrived, examined him and lifted him back to bed. But there was another fall around 8 AM and again the paramedics came. This time they deemed he should be taken to Margate hospital, and passively, he agreed.

We spent a lot of time sitting around waiting for assessments, while Dick looked mildly confused. Eventually, they said he should be kept in hospital: there was an infection and he needed further medical examinations. I drove back and forth twice that day and finally came back to our house, which had been named 'Villa Vita' by a previous owner (but which I had privately re-named 'In Which I Serve')where I was alone. 'Perhaps it's ignoble to confess this,' I wrote in my diary the next day. 'But it has been blissfully peaceful. I have never regarded this home to be mine, because I regard my time here as being in service. I must always serve Dick's needs.' Now the space was mine for an uninterrupted night's sleep.

Richard hated being in hospital – modern hospitals are impersonal and soulless, and nurses are often offhand and patronising – oh, where are the Matrons of yore, to impose standards? – but it was deemed medically necessary. I saw him two or three times a day, but I still relished the peace of being home alone.

After some weeks in hospital, the final assessment came, towards the end of October in 2010. There was a meeting at the hospital to decide on Dick's future, led by the care manager of the local social services. I had a heavy cold – I had a series of heavy colds at this stage, accompanied by a hacking cough – and Amanda Potter, the social services chief, said that in her view caring for Dick at home would be too much for me at the present time, and it was her advice that he should enter residential care.

And thus it was that my husband was transferred to a residential care home about half a mile from our house. I felt sad – has it come to this? Dick in an old folks' home? But I also felt relieved that the decision had been taken out of my hands. The social services made the decision, I reminded myself. And I also felt worried about my own health: I was, at the same time, due to have a series of chest x-rays and bronchial investiagations because of my hacking cough and persistant colds and breathlessness. I was 'a bout de souffle', in the title of that fascinating 1960 movie with Belmondo and Seberg: 'a bout de souffle' can be 'breathless': it can also be 'at the end of my tether.'

Richard seemed a bit dazed by it all.

Shortly after he was admitted, I went to see him, reporting that there was snow outside, and it was very cold. 'Then why did you go out?' he asked me. 'Well, to come here.' 'But you're staying at the same hotel, aren't you?'

He said he wanted to get up and walk. 'But, my dear, you can't walk at the moment,' I said, trying to be gentle. 'I *can* walk,' he protested. Later he would say that I was 'part of the conspiracy', pretending that he couldn't walk. He still occasionally imagines that he could perfectly well get onto his feet.

* * *

My health troubled me in 2011. I constantly seemed to have something wrong with me: digestive problems, stomach problems, eczema and psoriasis – my body was covered in rashes – arthritis in the neck, mysterious attacks of neuralgia and colds I found difficult to shake off, as well as two prosthetic hip-points, and knees beginning to go wobbly. I'd wake up in the middle of the night, wondering if I would catch my breath, and go to bed wondering if the night 'would take my breath away' – oh, that laburnum tree!

Yet I couldn't rest easily if Dick felt abandoned in the care home, even though I'd visit him every day. I'd have him home at weekends: I wanted him to have some home life, and to know that his family was still there for him. He complained of being 'dumped', and would say 'get me out of here'. This made me feel uncomfortably guilty, although Mrs Patel, the beautiful Indian woman who owned the care home, sought to dissuade me from having him out at the weekends. 'You have a good quality of life – but you'll wear yourself out caring for him yourself. Leave the heavy lifting to my staff. Take him out for lunch now and then.' It was the perfect utilitarian argument: why should two people have to have a miserable life when only one is obliged to do so?

But still, although it was a struggle, and incurred extra expense – there was no discount for his absences from the care home and I had to hire carers to help me get him up, toiletted and dressed – I still felt I should do what I could for him. When I'd deliver him back to the care home on a Monday, via a wheelchair-friendly taxi, I'd explain: 'Dick, dear, you must understand that I'm not able to care for you all the time, but it's lovely having you home part of the time.' All the same, inwardly, I'd breathe a sigh of relief as I drove away.

I've read many critical reports of care homes for the elderly and infirm, but I cannot disparage the residential home where Dick stayed during 2011 and 2012. Its material standards seemed to me to be excellent – everything was clean and well-run – and the staff were kind and obliging: in some cases especially patient, sunny-natured and helpful.*

---

*A care worker who subsequently left this employ complained that standards were not up to par. But all care homes, so far as I can judge, share the same problem: there is no intellectual stimulation – and neither the time nor the opportunity to create any.

As it happens, I spent a week in an old ladies' home myself in 2008, convalescing after a hip operation. It was clean and well-run, the location was pretty and the food was perfectly nice. But it was deadening from the point of view of mental stimulus. Only on the last day of a week's sojourn did I discover that my normally silent neighbour at table had been in the WRAF during the Second World War, and worked on radar with Battle of Britain pilots. Yet there was nothing in that environment which would have reflected her intelligence and accomplishments – and fascinating memories.

Richard's care home was similar: the day-room featured groups of old people seated around in a square formation. Some were perfectly *compos mentis*, but some had dementia problems; one old man who was seated near to Dick was constantly calling out for his mother – 'Mamma! Mamma!' – and whenever I would appear, he seemed to think that I was his mother, and would beg me piteously to come and help him, sometimes catching at my arm as I passed. There were mismatches in the seating arrangements. Rough old chaps who harrumped at the top of their voices were placed in proximity to genteel old ladies who were once aces at a cryptic crossword, or did something bookish at Oxford.

This is a description of the way things are: it is not a criticism of the standards maintained. But there might be a good business opportunity, one day, for someone to start up an old folks' home where there is mental stimulation: where old chaps play chess – or the cello; where cultured music is heard, not just a constant diet of pop drivel and facetious chatter; or where high-minded lectures and discourses are heard; where singers come and perform arias from the opera and some kindly soul visits each day to read from the literary journals. (I laughed like a drain when I saw the movie, *Quartet*, in which Maggie Smith and Billy Connolly are residents in such a care home – fantasyland, indeed.)

Dick was sometimes patient and accepting, sometimes grouchy and bad-tempered, sometimes in denial. He constantly claimed that he could get up and walk to the loo. He repeatedly said he could walk to a shower, if someone would just 'give him a hand'. He sometimes accused me of 'being part of the conspiracy', and harking back to merrier times when we had lively, but generally amicable, discussions about the Catholic-Protestant divide, he'd say more darkly that I was 'an agent for Vatican intelligence'.

'He's grieving for the life he once had,' said one of the nursing staff.

I'd visit him usually twice a day, plying him with freshly-brewed coffee in a thermos (no institution provides real coffee), biscuits, sherry, the papers, a CD. But after 2010, and that time in hospital, he ceased reading – which had been a lifelong pleasure. The eye specialist said that, although he was very myopic, he could read, but something in the eye and the brain didn't connect any more. He would just turn the pages of what were once enjoyable sources of reading. Even *Private Eye* remained unread.

And sometimes I'd come upon him in the main lounge, where he was sitting like Rodin's 'The Thinker', looking utterly wretched, and I'd feel such a surge of pity and guilt. Then I'd be plunged into depression again, and I'd go off to St Margaret's Bay, nearby, from where the white cliffs of Calais can be seen with shimmering clarity and whiteness. I'd just sit there, looking out over the Channel, brooding. Like Dick, I too was mourning for the life I once had. There was France! The beginning of the Continent! Liberty!

One day, listening to the car radio, I heard the actor Bill Nighy complain that people in old folks' homes were 'drugged up to the eyeballs'. If only they were! What better time in life – when you are very old, infirm, and often in pain – to be 'drugged up to the eyeballs?' Sometimes, entering the care home, I would hear the screams of 'Help! Help!' from a poor demented woman on the ground floor. Why shouldn't she be medicated, and heavily, if it would calm her appalling cries? Not only for her own distress, but for that of others.

(I sometimes thought if I could score a dose of heroin for Richard, and if it would make him content – and it does calm people down, and make them feel comforted – then I would.) But my experience is that the elderly infirm are, if anything, under-medicalised. Richard's medication, which I would dole out at the weekends, was rather minimal, it seemed to me. When I had the task of picking up his repeat prescriptions (for an antistroke drug, and a codeine-based painkiller), I found the local pharmacy sparing and austere about distribution: small amounts at a time, and I would be made to wait while everything was checked and controlled. Were they worried I would kill him with an overdose?

* * *

Occasionally, I would meet other women visiting their elderly and infirm husbands at the care home, and we'd talk in the entrance or exchange a few words in the car park. They all put on a brave face, though I knew they, too, found the whole situation painful and difficult. Men who had once been domineering were now needy and clinging, asking day and night for the attention of their long-suffering spouses. (Jack's frantic cry of 'Mamma! Mamma!' was, I discovered later, for his wife, not his mother. When I subsequently heard that Jack had died, in his mid-nineties, I was glad he had been delivered from his state of continual anxiety.)

One wife, who I'll call Anne, said her Catholic faith kept her going, but she still found it tough. Jeff, would stand by the door of the care home, one shoe off and one shoe on, waiting for her daily visits. Once a robust man and sure of himself, he was now pitifully needy.

Her husband had children by a previous marriage, but they never visited. 'Tell them it's their duty,' I suggested. 'No,' said Anne. 'No good doing it out of "duty". Do it out of love, or don't do it at all.' Anne had been an only child, and cared for her own elderly parents in their last years; her husband Jeff was also an only child, and she cared for his parents at the end of life, plus an elderly maiden aunt of Jeff's too. Almost her whole life, from her forties, had been taken up with care. There, indeed, was a saint. Or, was it martyrdom?

You hear of many remarkably unselfish people in this realm of caring, and many individuals who are visited with Job-like sufferings, too. A woman of forty – a friend of a friend - had a late baby, which was disabled. Then her husband had a stroke, and then both her parents fell ill, and she was caring for all of them – the baby, the husband, the parents.

I encountered women who gave up their jobs, overnight, to care for a partner, to whom they weren't married (and to whom they had made none of those sonorous vows), simply putting aside their own life overnight to dedicate themselves to the disabled one. Patsy, a lovely, lively Scotswoman I knew who had a fabulous job with airport control, simply dropped everything when her boyfriend Kevin had a stroke – so as to dedicate herself to nursing him. 'I could walk away,' she said. 'But I wouldn't.'

I occasionally talk to a pleasant Scandinavian writer of my own vintage who quit writing when her husband had a stroke. 'Every day there's so much to do for him – I can't do both my own work and the care,' she said. Yet, although she loves him and wants to do it, she does feel, sometimes, that it's all so relentless. Her husband is incapacitated but he can walk, very very slowly, so she hardly ever leaves his side. One day I met her in the street and she said – 'I wish he had some pals who would come and take him out.' Their grown offspring were scattered and the marriage had always been close. He had never been the kind of man who had gone off to the pub with mates, and now she rather wished he had done. The intense closeness of a good marriage may mean that other people tend to be excluded.

Is this a feminist issue, I asked myself? Is it simply that women are expected, or expect themselves, to sacrifice their lives when a spouse is ill? Or is it an issue of humanity? I can think of men who have done similarly – though in the nature of things, not so frequently as women, since women usually outlive men.

But so many women, despite the difficulties, seem ready to assume this caring role. My own struggle lies partly in the fact that I am not a self-sac-rificing individual by natural disposition; I do not share, perhaps, the more altruistic nature of many women – and I wonder if the fundamental femi-nist struggle is *against* the altruistic element in feminine nature. Perhaps equality between men and women will only ever be accomplished when women completely squash, within themselves, the caring impulse, which may indeed be linked to the maternal instinct.

One wife, Tricia Gannaway, exemplified this Mother Courage template, when she described, in the *Daily Mail*, her experience of caring for her husband, Charlie, also disabled from a stroke: 'I feared I would be too squeamish to carry out the daily tasks – some highly personal, many requiring endless patience and skills I was afraid I did not have – that Charlie could no longer accomplish himself.

'But a surprising strength and competence came over me. Just as a new mum deals intuitively with the needs of her baby, I discovered a capacity for care I didn't know that I possessed. And actually the menial tasks – the blanket baths, the washing and feeding – I did for Charlie in the first weeks of his recuperation were uplifting. I found there was no loss of dignity on either part. On the contrary, there is even a delight in caring so intimately for someone you love and once I realised that nothing fazed me, everything became much easier.'

I could identify with some of what Mrs Gannaway said (in an interview with the journalist Frances Hardy), the 'menial tasks' didn't worry me either. The personal care didn't worry me. There can, indeed, be a real satisfaction in seeing that someone you love is clean, fed, comfortable – and that you have made him comfortable.

The physical side of caring is not the hard bit: the hard bit is the loss of freedom, the absolute tie, the relentlessness of the duty, and that, in a basic sense, you can no longer call your life your own. It's the old feminist point: autonomy. Your autonomy has gone, and perhaps it's a pointer in time: autonomy goes with age and inevitable infirmity anyway.

Tricia Gannaway didn't resent this. 'I did not for a second resent the encroachment on my freedom; neither was I irked by Charlie's dependence. For the fact is – I would rather be his constant companion and carer than not have him at all.' Although constant companion to an invalid is a different situation than a constant companion to a functioning partner.

My friend Marjorie Wallace, who was caring for her partner Tom Margerison was also, I thought, saintly. Marjorie has cared for Tom for as long as I have looked after Richard – Tom has Parkinson's Disease and is quite helpless. She feels exactly like Tricia Gannaway: she would much rather be Tom's carer than be without him (though she does have excellent, and round-the-clock professional help too). One frantic evening in 2011, Tom was taken ill, and rushed to hospital in Highgate. There was concern about his heartbeat, which had become exceptionally slow. The medics thought he might be at the end of life. Marjorie sat up all night with him, and when a doctor asked her if all efforts should be made to revive him, if he slipped into unconsciousness, she insisted 'yes, yes, all efforts to keep him alive.'

I am supposed to be a pro-life Catholic, but that is not the decision I would make. I would say in these circumstances: 'Let nature take its course.'

Euthanasia often arose – and arises – in the media, and indeed in the courts, in both Ireland and Britain, where 'right to die' cases became a trend, as did the fashion for going to Switzerland to be legally euthanased at the termination clinic called Dignitas. Marjorie was very droll about that. 'Have you seen the *curtains* there?' she cried. 'My dear - imagine choosing to die amongst such tasteless, beige drapes!' Quite so.

Dick and I had spoken about this issue of assisted suicide in times gone by, when he was in the full of his health. Being a vague Anglican, he would take a basic Judeo-Christian approach to ethics, without being too vehement. But he certainly was against euthanasia when we had discussed it. 'Asking for trouble,' he'd say. Apart from the ethics, think of the disputed wills, the lawyers' arguments, the family quarrels – all bad enough, in the annals of family history, even without 'assisted suicide' issues. Dogs and cats are mercifully put down, for sure, when they suffer; but pets don't have the financial affairs to put in order, estates to divide up, wills to favour this or that family member.

My own view, though rooted in Catholic values, was nonetheless best summed up by the Victorian couplet, originally written ironically:

> *Thou shalt not kill, but needst not strive*
> *Officiously to keep alive.*

But by 2011, Richard was himself making ironic allusions to mercy killing. 'What would you like – a cup of coffee? A sherry?' He'd reply 'A glass of hemlock.' Other replies included 'a humane killer' and 'a loaded revolver'.

It was easy enough for the writer Will Self to deliver himself of a caustic discourse on BBC Radio 4's *A Point of View* virtually advocating mass euthanasia. We were often informed, he said with his lugubrious delivery, that we were suffering from 'an epidemic of cancer', and 'an epidemic of dementia'. No we weren't, he went on – we were suffering from an epidemic of old age. He came pretty near to advocating a 'humane killer' for the general population of the aged, and stated his intention of doing away with himself when the time of infirmity came near. Honest talk, maybe, but loose talk, too. The danger in advancing euthanasia is that it might prove such a temptation, especially when we get to the demographic point where there are too many old people and their numbers are a widespread burden on their families and communities.

It seems a hard-hearted point, but I can indeed think of cases where individuals wish to heaven that their elderly caree would die: old parents who go on and on, blighting the remaining years of their offspring themselves in their sixties and seventies. And that Yeats quotation really does reflect how long-serving daughters and sons can feel. I can think of a contemporary of mine who is not in good health himself, and still he has the burden of both parents, both in their nineties, and both afflicted with dementia. I know daughters in their sixties still ministering – often with frustration and exasperation – to their querulous mothers in their nineties. The experience, one friend told me, had turned her into 'hard-hearted Hannah'.

I do not always applaud when I hear medical specialists confidently predict that people will be living so much longer in the future: when the *National Geographic* magazine ran a report in 2013 saying that in times to come, humans would live to 140, I thought '*quelle horreur!*' Who will care for all these extremely old people? (Answer: just slightly younger old people.)

Yet the difference between 'let nature take its course' and 'the right to die' is a vast gulf. Advocates of the right to die fill my Facebook page with compassionate pleas for deliverance for those with long, interminable, afflicting and crippling illnesses. It is a 'human right': it is an 'individual choice': why should individuals be denied that choice because of an old religious prohibition? Again, what I think such advocates do not quite grasp is the temptation that would obtain, were all taboos and stigmas removed against such termination of life.

The uselessness of so much of extreme old age must surely propel more people into killing off the old and useless, were it an acceptable procedure: it is not a coincidence that every now and again comes a report about a nurse in a care home poisoning a clatter of oldies. The thought will often strike those professional carers that these lives are low on what is known as 'quality lifetime'. 'Life unworthy of living' was a phrase coined in the Third Reich: *lebensunwertesleben*. Much life must seem like that, but can we cross that frontier? It's the *temptation* that disturbs me. To put it more personally, if I had the possibility of giving Dick a painless overdose, and certain that I would neither be found out nor prosecuted, would I be tempted to do it? Yes, I would be tempted, but Catholic guilt would restrain me, once again. And in this one I would perhaps be grateful for Catholic guilt.

Part of the temptation to a widening policy of 'assisted suicide' is the money question. At the care home where my husband resided, he paid almost £3,000 a month, and individuals are expected to be self-funding until they have a minimum deposit of revenue left. It costs a sizeable amount of money to keep infirm and elderly people alive.

* * *

In 2012, I was diagnosed with a lung condition called bronchiectasis, which is classed as a Chronic Obstructive Pulmonary Disease. It can be reasonably well managed, but the breathlessness, chesty catarrah and sweats were endemic.

Yet once diagnosed, the condition was better controlled, thanks to the Brompton Hospital in dear old Chelsea, and I began to feel more energetic. If we could just move house – go somewhere bigger, which would accommodate all the paraphernalia an invalid requires: the medical bed, the wheelchair, commode, hoist, orthopaedic chair – we could bring Richard home. He came to accept being in the care home, but often looked miserable. And there was another reason: the cost of residential care. We were obliged to be self-funding, because Richard had some funds in a trust. But the money wouldn't last another year.

And so with the help (both practical and financial) of our son Patrick, a house move – the fifth since the stroke – was arranged, and on 1 February 2013, I duly brought Dick home, from which time I became his full-time carer, with support from agency staff. I was advised against taking this on by friends and some family members – my niece Marie-Louise, whose judgement I trust, told me I had a 'martyr complex'. I was warned that it was 'a huge undertaking'. Yet I felt it had to be done.

I once interviewed an elderly French nun (who had run errands for the Resistance as a young girl) who spoke about her vocation to the religious life when she was in her twenties. 'Something is pushing you,' she recalled.

Yes: there are times in your life when you do things for just this reason – something is pushing you. Sometimes it's an instinctive thing, like getting pregnant at a certain age; you wake up one morning and think 'this I must do'. Sometimes it's a matter of conscience, or even, possibly a 'higher power' (however you define that).

In early 2013, after our house move – always a major undertaking – I felt it was right to bring Dick home and take care of him full-time. It was time. I was now able to do it, so now is when I should do it. Perhaps I had also come to a point of acceptance. For years, I had kicked against my fate, of Minding Dick. Now, coming up to my seventieth year, perhaps it was time to practise acceptance. He had been obliged to practise acceptance. He hated giving up the life he had loved as a roving writer. He had often feared that phrase from the Bible: 'The night will come when no man will work.'

And to be truthful, being the full-on carer certainly is demanding, even with the back-up care and others helping out, including Patrick. The responsibility is still mine and will be for what remains of my life. Each day, my first and last thought has to be about Minding Dick.

I awake each morning around 6.40, so as to get an hour of reading and writing done before the care duties of the day begin. The agency care-worker arrives at 8.30 AM, and we wash, change and dress Dick, and move him, via a hoist, from his special orthopaedic bed to his special orthopaedic chair. Dick accepts these ministrations with great dignity, and sometimes even humour, and I admire his almost Zen attitude of just rising above it all. The agency careworkers appear three times a day to move the patient and change pads.

I give him breakfast in the morning, and then leave him for a short time to go and get the newspapers and other morning shopping errands. I read him extracts from a paper, and then, if there is something decent on TV (thank heaven for repeats of the ever-witty *Frasier*) I grab time to do a little more writing. Then there is coffee, and lunch, and related care issues to be attended to: contact the district nurse about seeing to pressure sores; drive to the pharmacy to pick up fresh medication; organise the meals, the outings (where possible – going out is problematic) and the general household arrangements. I have struggled to get Dick organised to go out – there has to be a male care assistant strong enough to help out with that – and it has involved more adaptations to the house.

In many ways, I am re-living some of the pattern of life when my children were little, when, like other mothers with jobs and careers, I tried to juggle a working life with a home life. I would try to meet a deadline before rushing back to fetch the child, or children, from nursery, and later, from school: it is a form of regret that 'career women', as they were termed, of my generation spent so much of their children's early years dashing around making childcare arrangements, instead of being able to enjoy our children, for childhood passes so quickly.

And now I am going through the reprise: struggling to get working deadlines squeezed into the time between caring for Dick, or arranging his care. Except that now I am heading for seventy, and we are both in decline. The vista of the future which sent me into a temporarily suicidal depression around 2004, on that road to Tunbridge Wells, has turned out to be altogether accurate: I did spend the last productive years of my life with this responsibility, around which everything else has to be organised.

When I feel trapped, and unhappy, I reflect that many people have worse crosses, God knows. I watch mothers wheeling very sick children or young people whose limbs are twisted from some dreadful disability, and consider what it would be to be in that situation. I have been spared to live a longer life than many of my friends, and I should be grateful for that. I've been thwarted in some of my ambitions by my caring role – I had to let drop a project which involved writing a book about France, although, to his credit, Dick wanted to come along with me and help (on the initial research trip to Rheims, for it involved a biography of the champagne queen, Madame Veuve Cliquot, so much time was taken in caring for him that it really turned out to be a fiasco.) I also had to drop out of a Masters Degree in Drama, for which I was accepted, at Goldsmith's College in London – twice: I deferred from 2011 to 2012, but it was impossible to attend a university three days a week, with my responsibilities.

But on the other hand, I've managed to write other books, and if I feel Dick's care has prevented me from doing things I wanted to do, he has always been warmly encouraging to me in my ambitions.

I have learned a lot about myself, himself, and others . . . I have learned that you never, ever say to an invalid – 'Is that more comfortable?' Or 'Are you feeling better now?' They are never feeling better – they are almost always in pain. Just as Dr Spock advised in his original book on baby care, it is always better to distract the caree with something positive, something promising. So it's not – 'Are you feeling more comfortable?' – but, rather 'let me get you a coffee/a sherry/a painkiller', or 'I think there's an old David Lean movie coming up.'

And I'm glad, too, that I'm a sufficiently accomplished actress – my gifts as an actress are not for the theatre but for real life – to have been able to conceal from Dick, all these years, my misery and frustration at being cast in the role of his carer. Hypocrisy, said Oscar Wilde, was the tribute that vice paid to virtue: I think I would prefer the more instrumental hypocrisy given as advice by the world's best counselling service, Alcoholics Anonymous – *Fake it till you make it!* Aspire to do the right thing, and if you don't feel happy inside, well, fake it till you make it . . . Telling the bald truth can often be cruel, and I am thankful I have never blurted out how imprisoned, frustrated and miserable I have often felt, since he was afflicted by the stroke. (Dick has, alas, lost the capacity to read now, so he will never read this, and I trust that no unkind person will read it to him.)

But I think it is important that carers should feel entitled to admit to the anger, resentment, frustration and depression that can come with this role; not to hurt the caree's feelings, ever, but to understand that there is self-sacrifice involved, and it is not always uplifting: sometimes it's wretched. And yet I am constantly impressed by the grace some carers show. Bruce Arnold loves looking after Mavis; Marjorie finds caring for Tom the most rewarding aspect of her life.

My daily caring duties come to an end about 8.30 PM, after the carer and I have put Richard to bed. I am always glad when another day is over. I am aware that this is what my mother called 'wishing your life away', and that is something one might regret at the end of life, but alas, that is how it is, and I have come to accept it.

* * *

I hoped he would be happier at home with us, and in some ways, I think he has been – happier isn't the word – but more serene. He has stopped asking for a chalice of hemlock or a loaded revolver, although there is the occasional allusion to departing this world. 'Pain killer?' I said the other day, and he echoed: 'Humane killer?' Struggling with his movable chair, I cried in exasperation: 'This chair will be the death of me.' He replied, almost eagerly: 'Me first!'

He sometimes smiles, and occasionally, even laughs (when I read to him Byron Rogers' recollection of Michael Wharton 'Peter Simple' in the *Spectator* – it brought back hilarious Fleet Street days). We do the things together that we never did in our salad days: listen to music together, watch old movies, and I read aloud to him – the *Daily Telegraph* obituaries, especially of eccentrics, old Battle of Britain pilots (they live an awfully long time if they survive 1940) and central European nobility are usually a great read, being mini-biographies. Anyway, old people have always enjoyed death notices. They capture the past, recall people one has known, or known of, or wishes one has known, and also reassure the reader that so far, it hasn't been quite our turn.

Perhaps in old age, and infirmity, I have learned that marriage is not really about 'autonomy', and he has had to learn that the freedom of independence of going hither and thither as you please – as in the old pub-going times – comes to an end.

His old friends remember him, but to be honest, he seldom gets any visitors now. I think it is mixture of things: the move from London meant that he lost contact with many of his old pals there. And then, some of them died – Tony Howard had sent a message that he was planning a trip just before he suddenly died in December 2010. He has had visits in the past from old friends like Geoffrey Wheatcroft, Neal Ascherson and Trevor Grundy, and people do remember Dick with affection. At a *Spectator* party a couple of years ago, lots of old friends asked after Dick – Ferdy Mount, Patrick Marnham, the cartoonist Michael Heath, who said, 'I love that man. I think of him every day.' Indeed, over the years many pals would ask 'How is Dick?' And when I would reply, 'really rather infirm'. 'Oh dear,' people would say. 'Give him my best regards.'

Sometimes friends have found him unrewarding to visit, too. He can fall silent, 'going into his own bubble,' as Julie Steeples says. But I think it's all part of the condition of being very, very crippled, and so frequently in pain. The constant pain has abated somewhat with more codeine – opium that is – but I have learned that you never ask a disabled person 'are you comfortable now?' They never are.

And yet, there have been many blessings. My dear friend Miriam, who died in 2005, would often invoke the motto: 'Count your blessings.' No matter how difficult life seems to be – count your blessings. I shared a flat with Miriam when I first came to London: she was the friend of my youth – half-Russian Jewish, half-Ulster Protestant, and a unique mixture of the soulful and the practical. She regularly appears to me in dreams. When I experience 'the Miriam dream', I know I must count my blessings. And they have been many: I am so grateful for family and friends.

In 2008, our younger son Ed and his now wife, Emma Grove, became the parents to a darling daughter, Kitty. In 2010, their second daughter, the adorable Eleanor, was born, and these grandchildren are a great joy. At the end of July 2013, their son, James Carlos, was born – the names of my adorable late brothers. Dick responded to the news – 'Wonderful!' Ed and his family live in North London, which is a distance from Deal, but when they're able to visit, it's a terrific joy. And it's fantastic to spend time with them in London, when I can.

In 2008, too, we acquired a home help, Ann Smart, who has been kindness itself. And through Dick's infirmities, we have encountered many good people – the daily carer, Jade, is a sweetie, and so nice to Richard, as was Karen – a great person – and, indeed, others. Despite my being so tied, I have managed to maintain my writing career, by ducking and weaving and somehow finding a way to get the work done; and to keep going to Ireland – even if it's for one night, touching base with Ireland is the most nurturing experience.

Through the process of Richard's infirmity, there have been moments of grace and humour, and I am touched that he can still sometimes smile – and can sometimes come out with an impressive word, or a quote from Dante. His is the greater burden. But one of my early journalistic mentors, Donal Foley, used to say, so jokily, 'the auld dog for the hard road!', and indeed that applies to old age and the process of decline for all of us; we must try our best to be good-tempered old dogs at the end.

Because.

Because the world changed, and moved on.

Because experience kept creeping up on me and disproving my earlier theories.

Because John Maynard Keynes said: 'when the facts change, I change my mind – what do you do?'

Because I watched an abortion being performed at twenty-three weeks pregnancy and felt desperately upset by the experience.

Because a writer must alter and develop. You can't dwell in an eternal 1968, unless you want to remain frozen in time.

Because I became a mother, and it dawned on me that I was responsible for other lives.

Because I quit drinking and all that went with it.

Because I experienced the Soviet Union and East Germany up close and concluded that utopias seldom work.

Because I came to see, by experience, that humans are flawed creatures – the doctrine of original sin did, somehow, have a point.

Because the mother of sons perceives that sometimes it's hard to be a man. (*pace* Tammy Wynette).

Because I became interested in history and that brought different perspectives to experience.

Because Donal Foley said to me: 'it's just because you're beginning to realise how kind your family were.'

Because I began to understand that 'there is no such thing as a free lunch'.

(Or, as the Spanish proverb puts it: 'Take what you want, says God: and pay for it.')

Because you have to learn by your mistakes and blunders: 'try again, fail again, fail better'.

Because I read some biological science and accepted the evidence that not all gender inequality was 'social conditioning'. Hormones and chromosomes, not to mention brain wiring, are usually different in males and females. Not an excuse to disadvantage women, but sometimes an explanation of why few parliamentary democracies are voluntarily a 50/50 balance between the sexes.

Because, while I certainly continue to support the emancipation and liberation of women, I began to find obsessive feminism narrow and sectarian.

Because children are conservative by nature, and want a stable home life, with parents who make them feel safe, not wild hippies who live for kicks.

Because acquiring property has a strange effect of *embourgeoisement*.

Because young people should question the world they inherit, but older people should rescue what was good from that inheritance.

Because conformity comes in many guises: you can be a conformist radical as much you can be a conformist member of the bourgeoisie. But it's more important to find your true self ('become the person you truly are,' said Nietzsche) than to submit unthinkingly to any era's political correctness.

Because values that have lasted thousands of years probably are there for a reason.

Because I've seen lots of people made very unhappy by crazed sex-and-drugs-and-rock 'n' roll.

Because so much of what I thought I liked I gradually discovered was not to my true taste at all, and there had been a lot of self-delusion going on, from imagining that I was a good dancer to thinking I was dead sexy when I was just dead ridiculous.

Because 'there's been a load of compromisin'/ On the road to my horizons'.

Because we may denounce 'the authoritarian personality', yet the exercises of good authority is essential. I took a refresher course in French and felt a spontaneous wave of contempt when the teacher turned up in torn jeans and a sloppy tee-shirt. She had diminished her own authority.

Because I identified with Wendy Cope's poem about making disastrous choices: 'She never made the same mistake again/ She always made a new mistake instead.'

Because I look back on things I said and marvel: 'How could I have been so naive!'

Because one of the seven secrets of happiness (according to gurus) is: 'Don't resist change'.

Because once what was transgressive became mainstream, I lost interest. (Kids are being *taught* how to run a protest or demonstration; tourists in Dublin are being *guided* on a pub-crawl.)

Because at the age of thirty-two (research apparently says) a woman turns into her mother.

Because I read Auden's words with a chilling sense of recognition: 'Time will say nothing but I told you so/Time only knows the price we have to pay . . .'

Because the Hound of Heaven finally caught up with me.

Some of the reasons I give when asked why I changed from a fiery revolution-ary to a Burkean conservative: and some of them are even true.